DIPLOMACY AND THE ARCTIC COUNCIL

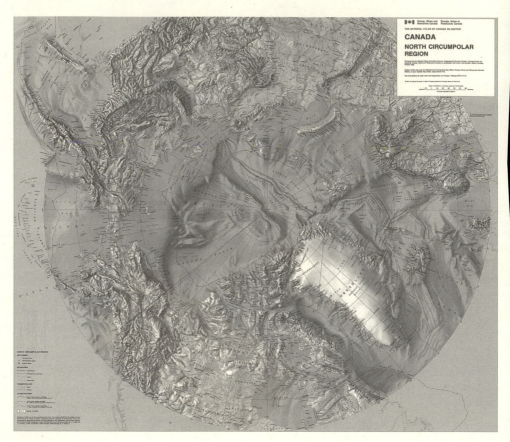

Map of the Arctic (Open Source from the Government of Canada)

Diplomacy and the Arctic Council

DANITA CATHERINE BURKE

McGill-Queen's University Press
Montreal & Kingston · London · Chicago

ISBN 978-0-7735-5918-9 (cloth)
ISBN 978-0-7735-5919-6 (paper)
ISBN 978-0-7735-5973-8 (ePDF)
ISBN 978-0-7735-5974-5 (ePUB)

Legal deposit fourth quarter 2019
Bibliothèque nationale du Québec

Printed in Canada on acid-free paper that is 100% ancient forest free
(100% post-consumer recycled), processed chlorine free

The research and publication of this book was supported by the
Carlsberg Foundation and the European Union's Horizon 2020
research and innovation programme. This project has received funding
from the Carlsberg Foundation as part of the Distinguished Postdoctoral Research Fellowship (Project Number: CF15-0434) and the European Union's Horizon 2020 research and innovation programme
under the Marie Skłodowska-Curie grant agreement No 746312.

Funded by the   Financé par le
Government   gouvernement
of Canada   du Canada

Canada

Canada Council   Conseil des arts
for the Arts   du Canada

We acknowledge the support of the Canada Council for the Arts.

Nous remercions le Conseil des arts du Canada de son soutien.

Library and Archives Canada Cataloguing in Publication

Title: Diplomacy and the Arctic Council / Danita Catherine Burke.
Names: Burke, Danita Catherine, author.
Description: Includes bibliographical references and index.
Identifiers: Canadiana (print) 20190183640 | Canadiana (ebook) 2019018373X |
    ISBN 9780773559196 (paper) | ISBN 9780773559189 (cloth) | ISBN 9780773559738
    (ePDF) | ISBN 9780773559745 (ePUB)
Subjects: LCSH: Arctic Council. | LCSH: International relations. | LCSH: Arctic
    regions—International status.
Classification: LCC KZ4110.P65 B87 2019 | DDC 341.4/4091632—dc23

This book was typeset by True to Type in 11/14 Sabon

Contents

Acknowledgments

This book is part of a larger project about diplomacy in the Arctic region and the Arctic Council. I would like to acknowledge and thank the many people who contributed to the completion of this project.

First, I would like to thank the Carlsberg Foundation, which funded the completion of the research from which this book is based, for their generous support of the project. This project also inspired the development of a new project on the role of environmental non-governmental organizations (ENGOs) in the Arctic region and their role in regional diplomacy. My project on ENGOs is funded by the European Union's Horizon 2020 research and innovation program under the Marie Skłodowska-Curie grant agreement No. 746312.

Second, I would like to thank all those people throughout the Arctic region who participated in my research as interviewees and gave me their time, attention, and support to undertake this project. The completion of this book, and the project, would not have been possible without their participation, transparency, and willingness to be part of the dialogue about international diplomacy and regional cooperation in the Arctic.

Third, I would like to thank those who helped in the hosting, preparation, and analysis of the project. Special thanks to my host institution, the Center for War Studies, University of Southern Denmark (SDU), and to my visiting scholar host institutions, the School of Political Studies, University of Ottawa, and the Department of Political and Economic Studies, University of Helsinki. Thank you to those who helped arrange these placements, in particular Sten Rynning and Vincent Keating (SDU), Christian Rouillard (Ottawa), and Juri Mykkänen (Helsinki). In addition, thank you to the Centre of Canadian Studies at the University of Edinburgh, Ilisimatusarfik/University of Greenland, the Arctic Politics Research Seminar group at the University of Copenhagen and Aalborg University, and the International Studies Research Unit at Cardiff University, all of which provided me with opportunities to present on aspects of the project's research.

Thank you, as well, to those who helped guide and advise me throughout the various stages of project preparation, in particular: Kai Striebinger, Frederik Harhoff, Maria Ackrén, Jenni Rinne, Veera Laine, and Arjen van Dalen. Additionally, from the Center for War Studies, SDU: Pål Røren, Sten Rynning, Vincent Keating, Peter Viggo Jakobsen, Chiara de Franco, and Olivier Schmitt. Similarly, I would like to thank Andre Saramago, Teale Phelps Bondaroff, and Jon Rahbek-Clemmensen, who worked with me on the completion of publications associated with the broader project.

Lastly, I would like to thank my family for their unwavering support throughout the project. Without their love and that support, the completion of this project would not have been possible.

DIPLOMACY AND THE ARCTIC COUNCIL

Introduction

During the Cold War, before the collapse of the Soviet Union, diplomatic relations in the Arctic were impeded by the region's strategic military value. By 1987, with Soviet leader Mikhail Gorbachev's Murmansk speech outlining the Soviet Union's foreign policy to establish a "zone of peace" in the Arctic (Åtland 2008a, 305–6), a process toward Arctic cooperation had begun to develop. Regional dialogue was initiated in non-military sectors such as "resource extraction, scientific exploration, Indigenous Peoples affairs, environmental protection and maritime transportation" (Åtland 2008a, 305). Illustrating the understanding that "diplomatic relations [are] the pre-condition for unhindered diplomacy," it was these first interactions on non-military issues that made way for the development of regional (Arctic) diplomacy and led to the eventual formation of the Arctic Council in 1996 (James 2016, 257).

Since then, the Arctic Council has facilitated more than twenty years of successful diplomacy and regional cooperation between Russia and the seven other Arctic states – Canada, the United States, Norway, the Kingdom of Denmark, Iceland, Sweden, and Finland. Of these eight states that have sovereignty over land within the Arctic Circle, those that have coastlines on the Arctic Ocean (Canada, the Kingdom of Denmark, Norway, Russia, and the United States) are considered "coastal states"; and the "non-coastal states" (Iceland, Sweden, and Finland) are those that have territory that intersects the Arctic Circle but no coastlines (or recognized coastlines) along the Arctic Ocean. In addition, there are six Permanent Participant Indigenous organizations (Aleut International Association, Arctic Athabaskan Council, Gwich'in Council International, Inuit Circumpolar Council, Russian Association of Indigenous Peoples of the North, and the Saami Council), which represent the Indigenous peoples who live throughout the region. Representatives of these Indigenous organizations have permanent access to, and actively participate in, the forum's diplomatic meetings, working groups, and task forces (Arctic Council 2015h). Unlike the eight Arctic states, however, the Permanent Participants do not have a formal say in final consensus decision-making.

When the Russian-Ukrainian conflict over the Crimea region erupted in 2014, serious concerns arose as to the implications of this conflict for Arctic cooperation. How would the military conflict affect the workings of the Arctic Council, a voluntary cooperation forum explicitly designed to exclude matters of military security? Since some of the council members were political players intimately involved in the Crimean conflict, these players needed to respond to that conflict through other avenues (despite their interest in issues directly relevant to the Arctic Council). Although Ukraine is not in the Arctic region, it is a partner state of the North Atlantic Treaty Organization (NATO), the defence treaty alliance originally set up to counteract the rise of communism and the security threat coming from the Soviet Union. All the Arctic states, with the exception of Russia, are either members or partner states of this alliance.

NATO members, along with other states, were concerned that the Ukraine conflict signalled an accelerating Russian aggression in international politics that could potentially spill over into the Arctic (Murray and Keating 2014). The events surrounding the Crimean conflict were linked to Russia's remilitarization, which began in the early 2000s during President Vladimir Putin's initial years in office (Laruelle 2014). Russia's remilitarization is seen as a key piece of that state's plan to regain the international status and respect it lost during the internal economic and social struggles that followed the collapse of the Soviet Union. It should be noted that this militarization has reportedly slowed down since 2017, due to Russia's continued financial difficulties (Blank 2017). When the conflict over the Crimea region broke out, international attention was focused on the deployment of troops on Europe's Eastern frontier, and news headlines drew parallels with the Cold War. A prominent Canadian newspaper, for instance, published an editorial titled "Cold War reply in Crimea" (*Globe and Mail* 2014, A10); the *New York Times* ran an article titled "If Not a Cold War, a Return to a Chilly Rivalry" (Baker 2014, 1); and a piece called "Old, familiar Cold War chills" appeared in New Zealand (*The Press* 2014, 16).

Bilateral relations with Russia, as well as multilateral relations within other forums and institutions, suffered substantially from the fallout of the conflict. Despite some disruptions, however, cooperation continued within the Arctic Council. How was this possible? How can it be accounted for? If we contextualize the conflict within the broader practices of Arctic cooperation and the reasons for the Arctic states initially coming together in the way they did, some clarity emerges. My hope is that this study of the Arctic Council will engender a stronger appreciation for why, despite the Ukraine conflict, cooperation has been maintained and continues in the Arctic region today.

An important clue is found in the concept of the "club." Bertrand Badie, in his *Diplomacy of Connivance*, has observed that a "club is constituted for the pleasure of its members, but under the circumstances, this obvious fact had to be carefully concealed." The circumstances he refers to are those that lead up to a club's formation (Badie 2012, 24). Building on Badie's notion of clubs, it appears that the Arctic Council is a club under the direction of the Arctic states and a high degree of input from Arctic Indigenous peoples, who collectively use the forum as a vessel to define and guide the parameters of their cooperation. As central club members, the Arctic states in particular act in ways that reflect the club's objectives, which they themselves have defined and which in turn reflect the internal hierarchies among the club state members. To gain some insight into how regional cooperation takes place through the Arctic Council, we must first acknowledge the intentions behind the club's formation.

The Arctic Council was established to address questions related to the Arctic environment and its development. As expressed and defined within the council's mandate, the shared intention of the Arctic states was to focus on the non-military issues of environmental protection and sustainable development. These focus areas reflect what members are willing to discuss in seeking shared solutions and opportunities, and have had the function of delineating discussions. The members designed the club and they run the club. A careful review of this context and the way the club has been managed and evolved over time may help explain how an event such as the 2014 Ukraine conflict, which pitted the NATO alliance and partner states against Russia, did not halt Arctic cooperation.

By looking into the club structures of the Arctic Council and the daily practices that occur within those structures and affect the relative status of its member-states, I hope to offer insight into the way the council addresses challenges and has been able to weather the storm of major international political events involving its core membership. The impression that the Arctic Council operates like a club has become more defined as international interest in the forum and in the Arctic region has grown in the past ten years (e.g., Rossi 2015). This increased interest has resulted in the Arctic states becoming more vigilant in their coordination and communication about their cooperation through the Arctic Council, and in turn helps to explain some of the club-like practices of the forum.

The declaration that created the Arctic Council and established its mandate is central to defining the club's existence, and from this point of departure we can gain a clearer sense of the formal and informal rules that have developed within the forum. Friction is introduced as a result of member-states navigating their roles and interests within the Arctic Council and pressures to adapt the forum's structure or amend the parameters of its mandated focus. Such friction is a recurring feature of daily diplomacy within the Arctic Council. At the same time, the broader international standing of the individual Arctic states also comes into play. All these factors shed light on the Arctic Council's practices – its internal practices, as well as its behaviour toward outside audiences and against outside pressures.

Unity is often the best defence in the face of external pressures from actors who want to insert themselves into the club's region or areas of focus and it has been the cornerstone of the Arctic Council's success. China is a prime example of a state seeking to extend its influence into the Arctic region. China is investing heavily in regional development, including mining in Iceland (e.g., Whigham 2016) and the development of the Northern Sea Route with Russia (e.g., Liu 2017). At the same time, China is promoting its Northern and Arctic credentials. In its 2018 White Paper, the Government of China stated that "China is an important stakeholder in Arctic affairs. Geographically, China is a 'Near-Arctic State,' one of the continental States that are closest to the Arctic Circle" (State Council Information Office of the People's Republic of China 2018). The combination of China's increased involvement in regional development and its growing tendency to articulate its vision of itself in the region, which at times opposes the views of some of the Arctic states, signals rising pressure and a challenge that the Arctic states must manage.

Maintaining regional unity requires a delicate balancing act that plays out among many actors both inside and outside the club. These actors include:

- the core members of club, in this case the Arctic states, who have the agency to formally direct the forum and its decision-making processes;
- the Permanent Participants, who have the ability to inform and influence the decision-making process without fear of losing their club membership, and who validate the legitimacy of the club;
- and conditional club members, who support the club's work through financial contributions and in-kind support such as scientific expertise, equipment for research, project personnel, and education opportunities, and who often make up the observer membership (e.g., Arctic Council 2015g). These members include:
  - non-governmental organizations (NGOs) such as the World Wide Fund for Nature – Global Arctic Program (WWF);
  - intergovernmental organizations (IGOs) such as the United Nations Environment Programme;

- non-Arctic states such as China, Germany, and India;
- and outside actors who do not have observer status, such as the European Union.

The balance in the cooperative relationship among these actors can be upset, for example, by national politicians and diplomats ignoring, or not understanding the (often unwritten) rules of behaviour that guide the dynamics of successful group practices within the club. In the case of the Arctic Council, maintaining unity among the permanent members involves numerous internally and externally focused practices performed at state-to-state and representative-to-representative levels.

This exploration of the daily practices of the Arctic Council helps us to see how daily challenges are identified and addressed. I draw upon the personal reflections and interpretations of the council's work from the perspective of current and former consultants and representatives such as Senior Arctic Officials, working group members, and chairpersons who participated in the forum, and diplomats posted to Arctic states. Underpinning my perspective is the view that the club format informs the dynamics of this diplomatic environment. I use the Arctic Council as an illustrative case to highlight how the practices of the diplomatic environment are informed by the structures and norms that have developed around its club dynamics.

Despite the Arctic states' efforts to insulate the Arctic Council from non-regional issues, the club (or forum) still faces pressures resulting from the relations between its members and their pursuit of sometimes conflicting interests. In attempting to understand how it was possible that Russia's actions in the Ukraine, for instance, did not completely derail Arctic cooperation within the Arctic Council, it becomes clear that the club's structure and practices, as well as the context in which these practices occur, play a significant role. As one high-ranking retired Arctic Council representative commented in relation to the conflict in the Crimea: "It reminds me that both the Brits and the Argentines came to the meeting on the Antarctic Treaty in 1983 despite the situation in the Falklands. There are certain things that go beyond nationalist concerns. And I submit that polar cooperation is one area where that's happened" (Retired Arctic Council chairperson, 7 June 2016).

The Ukraine conflict did have an impact on the Arctic Council, as this book will show, but the forum's work continued nevertheless. The conflict, however, did highlight and exacerbate some issues within the Arctic Council and opened the Arctic region's pre-eminent forum to further critique for its supposed shortcomings. As a result, the fallout from the Ukraine conflict had the unintended effect of refocusing the Arctic states on regional unity and reminding its core members about the importance of the role that the Arctic Council plays in projecting this unity. It helped the Arctic states and Indigenous organizations secure their status as the leaders in the management of the region.

THE ARCTIC COUNCIL IN THE LITERATURE

There is no shortage of literature on the Arctic Council available in current scholarship. Many works provide detailed back-stories about the formation of the forum, starting with Gorbachev's 1987 Murmansk Speech and the subsequent Finnish and Canadian initiatives over the next decade to develop a regional cooperation body (e.g., Nord 2016; English 2013; Keskitalo 2004). This background is important, but it generally covers a well-documented time period in the Arctic Council's history. Details about the forum's negotiations, such as its struggle to define "sustainable development" and its debate around the legal implications of describing the people in the Arctic as "Indigenous people versus Indigenous peoples," are equally well documented (e.g., Nord 2016; English 2013; Keskitalo 2004). Throughout this book I draw upon this body of work, which includes texts by authors such as John English and Douglas C. Nord, to contextualize the perceived current challenges faced by the Arctic Council. It is not necessary, however, to repeat a historical account of the development of the forum, from its negotiation in the late 1980s to mid-1990s until the present time (English 2013; Nord 2016).

While the Arctic Council is often promoted as the pre-eminent forum for Arctic regional discussions (Poelzer and Wilson 2014, 214), its pre-eminence has been called into question. According to Torbjørn Pedersen, "different theoretical traditions within the field of international relations studies" give rise to disagreement over the Arctic Council's importance (Pedersen 2012, 146). A range of opinions on the council's work have been expressed. A.H. Hoel, in "The Legal-Political Regime in the Arctic," states, for instance, that the Arctic Council is "the strongest institutionalization of cooperation in the pan-Arctic area" and "has facilitated a stable regional environment in the Arctic" (Hoel 2014, 62–3). Arctic scholars David VanderZwaag, Rob Huebert, and Stacey Ferrara, on the other hand, in their scholarly research on the Arctic Council and the Arctic Environmental Protection Strategy (AEPS), complain that the work of the Arctic Council has "largely involved studying and talking about environmental problems with little concrete action" (VanderZwaag et al. 2001, 226). In interviews I conducted for this book, many Arctic state representatives to the Arctic Council expressed the view that the Council is indeed a talk shop, but one aimed at keeping lines of communication open – a zone of peace – between the Arctic states on matters of the environment and development in the region (e.g., Representative to the Arctic Council, 10 May 2016). Terry Fenge and Bernard Funston, in their report for Greenpeace, speak of the Council as "an intergovernmental forum, but … not yet a fully mature entity" (Fenge and Funston 2015, 9).

Existing discussions about the work of the Arctic Council rarely go far enough in their exploration of the pressures and limitations of the diplomatic dynamics within the Arctic Council. As a result, the literature sometimes perpetuates far-reaching expectations about the forum, and what those assigned to work there can achieve. The general approach of this book, and my decision to focus on direct representative input, was inspired by two articles. The first was the journal article by Paula Kankaapää and Oran R. Young titled "The Effectiveness of the Arctic Council," which sought to "tap the knowledge of those in a position to articulate informed views regarding the activities of the council" (Kankaapää and Young 2012, 1). The Kankaapää and Young study served to identify general trends (Kankaapää and Young 2012, 2), which then created the demand for a more detailed (qualitative/ descriptive) analysis of these trends. This book builds on this approach. In relying on extensive in-depth interviews, I hope to generate an understanding of the functioning of the Arctic Council with greater richness and validity.

Kankaapää and Young's emphasis on the importance of hearing from practitioners and going directly "to elicit the views of people familiar with the council and its work" motivated my methodology, which is a change from the general methodology employed in the surge of Arctic scholarship in recent years. The term "permanent observer status" offers an excellent example of the disconnect in research and reporting about the Arctic Council. The term is inconsistently and unofficially applied and often appears in articles, statements, or news stories to describe an application for "permanent observer status" made to the Arctic Council. While the Arctic Council in its early years contributed to this confusion, it has distanced itself from the "permanent" observer label, which was unofficially used to contrast the observer membership of successful applicants for conditional membership with the ad hoc observers for limited periods of time that used to exist (also see Depledge 2015). The continued use of this language, however, by other actors and authors is problematic. Such language creates confusion about the Arctic Council and what participation in the observer status category means for observer applicants and members, and ultimately results in misrepresentation of the role of permanent observers in the council. *The Telegraph* (*The Telegraph* 2013), the *EU Observer* (Phillips 2009) and even the Republic of Korea's embassy in Sweden (Embassy of the Republic of Korea in the Kingdom of Sweden 2013), since South Korea became an observer member in 2013 (Arctic Council 2015g) – have all misrepresented what the observer status is, by calling it a "permanent status."

Documents and reports created by the Arctic states themselves are sometimes guilty of contributing to the confusion. For example, in the 2013 Canadian House of Commons "Report of the

Standing Committee on Foreign Affairs and International Development" for the 41st Parliament, 1st Session, the term "permanent observer" is used even though the Government of Canada does not label observers as permanent. In the committee report, under the heading "The Role of Non-Arctic States," it gives recommendations that Canada grant permanent observer status to China and the European Union (Report of the Standing Committee on Foreign Affairs and International Development 2013, 58), although it later undermines the notion of the "permanent" status it has been referring to by reminding readers that "permanent observer status will be reviewed every four years to ensure that the above-listed criteria [Nuuk criteria] are still being met by the party in question" (Report of the Standing Committee on Foreign Affairs and International Development 2013, 60). Such inconsistent language usage can create confusion about the Arctic Council, the position of the Arctic states, and what participation in it means for observer applicants and members, as well as the role of the Permanent Participants, who really are permanent members of the forum.

An implication of the misuse of the term is that it can feed into academic and policy paper reports. Andrew Chater, for instance, notes that observers are often referred to as "permanent observers," but that the Arctic Council refers to them as "accredited observers" without correcting the label (Chater 2015, 4) and he continues to use the term "permanent observer" throughout his piece (e.g., Chater 2015, 5, 26, 221). Julien Daemers, a law-of-the-sea specialist working for the Directorate for Strategic Affairs at the French Ministry of Defence, also wrote a paper in which he discusses the European Union's application "for a Permanent Observer Status within the [Arctic Council] ... [to] increase the legitimacy of the European Union as a relevant Arctic player" (Daemers 2012, 7). The fact is that formally, observers are not permanent; no such category exists. Observers apply for membership, are assessed by the Arctic states, who grant observer status by consensus decision, and subsequently monitor observer participation to evaluate their contributions to the club and adherence to the rules of procedures, to determine whether their membership continues. Ultimately, the incorrect use of the term "permanent observer" results in a misrepresentation of the role of observers and obscures the difference in their status compared to Permanent Participants in the council, thereby adding to international misunderstandings about Indigenous peoples in the Arctic and risking the dilution of their status and central importance in Arctic decision-making.

The second piece that inspired this book is an article written by Terry Fenge and Bernard Funston called "The Practice and Promise of the Arctic Council" (Fenge and Funston 2015). This independent report, which was produced for Greenpeace, provides a clear and accessible message about what the authors see as the internal and external challenges to the Arctic Council, while aiming to help inform Greenpeace members about the Arctic Council and dispel myths about the Arctic region. In light of Greenpeace's efforts to become more involved in Arctic politics, this article is extremely informative about common misconceptions about the Arctic held by people with little practical experience with the region's cooperation forum. One notable message throughout the piece is its aim to dispel the false belief that the Arctic, as a region, is a pristine, empty space that lacks a jurisdictional framework. Fenge and Funston's work gives brief explanations of different internal and external challenges that the Arctic Council faces. The present book goes beyond the introductory nature of their article and delves more deeply into the challenges that representatives to the Arctic Council and diplomats experienced when they reflected on and engaged with the forum.

In addition to the above-mentioned articles, other notable works have helped to inform this book; helping to triangulate the research and reflect on the debates about the strengths of and challenges faced by the Arctic Council. The existing literature focusing on the Arctic Council covers themes such as the history of the forum's formation and evolution (e.g., English 2013; Graczyk and Koivurova 2015); the push for institutional reform (e.g., Bergh 2012); the impact of Arctic Council chair leadership on chairmanship legacy (e.g., Exner-Pirot 2016); the perception of Arctic regional exceptionalism (e.g., Käpyla and Mikkola 2015); and the role of observers within the forum (e.g., Graczyk 2011).

More specifically, Annika E. Nilsson's 2012 piece "Knowing the Arctic: The Arctic Council as a Cognitive Forerunner" argues that the Arctic Council is a cognitive forerunner, acting as a soft-power entity, which has elevated the Arctic Council's political and geostrategic value (Nilsson 2012). However, Nilsson also critiques ongoing assessments of the forum's capabilities. Nilsson highlights, for example, that "the political challenges in reaching legally binding political agreements" continue to be an issue. Some of interviewees I spoke to during my fieldwork for this book echo Nilsson's conclusions that "the current organizational structure [of the Arctic Council] is not adequate for the challenges that are facing the Arctic today" (Nilsson 2012, 191). Nilsson's analysis, however, focuses heavily on the work of one of the six Arctic Council working groups, the Arctic Monitoring and Assessment Programme (AMAP), and uses only a select few interviews for its primary research (Nilsson 2012, 195–6). Her work provides a tantalizing glimpse into the dynamics of the Arctic Council. This book expands on Nilsson's exploration of the council's working dynamics by offering a more macro–Arctic Council perspective on the forum's strengths and challenges by studying both the structure of the club and the practices within it.

In this book I also draw on Arctic literature within the fields of international relations, political science, human geography, history, Indigenous studies, law, and biology. This broad array of literature reflects various common themes that were raised during my conversations with state and Permanent Participant representatives, diplomats, researchers, and academics which constituted the fieldwork component of the research for this book. These themes range from:

- the influence of domestic Arctic nationalism and identity on states' approaches to Council cooperation (e.g., Burke 2017b; Burke 2018; Medby 2014; Rowe 2016);
- the legacy and impacts of the environmental degradation of the Arctic region, particularly in the former Soviet Union (e.g., Kirchner 2000);

- the implications of climate change on the Arctic environment (e.g., Kutz et al. 2005);
- the role of Indigenous peoples within Arctic politics and the Arctic Council (e.g., Greaves 2015; Shadian 2010; Loukacheva 2009; Tennberg 2010);
- disputes over what qualifies a state to be labelled as an Arctic coastal state (e.g., Dodds and Ingimundarson 2012);
- how military-related challenges and threats, both globally and within the Arctic region influence perceptions of cooperation (e.g., Åtland 2008b, also see Inge and Findley 2006);
- Russia's resurgence in the region and the implications of this resurgence on cooperation in the Arctic region (e.g., Klimenko 2016; Käpylä et al. 2016); and
- the growth of non-Arctic state interest in the Arctic region (e.g., Jakobson and Peng 2012; Jakobson 2010).

The themes raised in this literature serve to contextualize responses given during my conversations with interviewees, and to assist with the analysis of the responses of those interviews.

OUTLINE

Chapter 1 establishes the theoretical framework which serves as the foundation of the book, as well as details the methodology employed. It begins with a discussion of status, and how the pursuit of status influences diplomacy. An understanding the role of "status" and its influence on diplomacy underlies the theoretical framework of this book. The pursuit of status and efforts taken to maintain status are at the heart of why clubs like the Arctic Council operate as they do. Building on the concept of the Arctic Council as a club, the chapter then moves on to explore club diplomacy in international politics through the work of Bertrand Badie. Badie helps to categorize the structure of the Arctic Council, and the broader diplomatic environmental within which the forum was created, and within which it currently operates.

The first chapter then meshes the discussion about club diplomacy with an examination of multilateral diplomacy and "pecking orders," paying particular attention to Vincent Pouliot's work on "practices" (e.g., Pouliot 2016a, 2016b). This analysis provides an in-depth examination of the internal and external diplomatic dynamics of Arctic politics, using the Arctic Council as the nexus of this diplomatic discussion. In this chapter I argue that the dynamics of regional politics and cooperation in the Arctic reflect the existence of diplomatic pecking orders and international status hierarchies. As a result, the state delegates to the Arctic Council work to maintain their states' respective positions within the forum, as well as to maintain the forum's overall position at the top of the international status hierarchy for non-military issues and interests in the Arctic.

To understand how the Arctic state representatives manage these major undertakings, I look to the daily, though seemingly mundane, practices of forums and institutions. It is through the careful study of the routine challenges faced by people trying to overcome these daily challenges that we can observe diplomatic dynamics in play.

The remainder of the book applies the framework presented in chapter 1 to the empirical examination of diplomacy in the Arctic Council. This analysis is presented in two parts. Each part explores challenges to Arctic Council cooperation, with Part One exploring internal challenges, and Part Two exploring external challenges. I have divided the book in this fashion, with the intention of highlighting the nuanced ways in which the club members act toward each other, as compared with their behaviours when dealing with outside pressures and actors.

The four chapters of Part One discuss the key internal challenges identified through the fieldwork conducted as part of the research for this book. It starts, in chapter 2, with an evaluation of funding, which is the challenge most frequently identified by interviewees. Funding is a pivotal factor influencing the forum's cooperation dynamics and the most complex challenge to address.

Chapter 3 turns to the challenge of institutional memory and knowledge depreciation. Institutional memory is a core challenge to successful regional cooperation as a result of the Arctic Council's structures and practices, as well as the structure and practices of individual delegations. This is also a challenge that cannot be addressed by the Council alone, despite the substantial efforts to address it through the creation of the Arctic Council Secretariat. As a result, this chapter reflects on the broader influences that the Arctic states and Permanent Participants have, and can have, on the forum's institutional memory.

The following chapter focuses on the issue of leadership, mainly the role of the chair and the need to minimize the temptation to use leadership opportunities in the forum as a platform to play out national politics on the international stage. Here the example of Canada's domestic politics creeping into its chairmanship during the Ukraine conflict is used to illustrate this issue.

Lastly, the fifth chapter narrows in on the specific challenge of language barriers. Despite being seen by the seven Western Arctic states as a central arena for engaging Russia, the forum operates primarily in English, thereby presenting a challenge to diplomatic relations. This chapter shows that the ways in which the issue of language barriers is managed is illustrative of club priorities and status politics between the Arctic states. Through the exploration of language barriers, this chapter examines Russia's elevated status and Norway's pivotal role in brokering regional cooperation.

Part Two is more outward-looking. It begins with chapter 6 and its study of two interrelated external challenges: communication about, and from, the Arctic Council and its work, and misunderstandings about the governance of the Arctic and the role of the Arctic Council in this region. These are major issues with which the Arctic Council and the Arctic states have struggled. They contribute to the development of scepticism about the forum and give rise to challenges as to whether it is indeed the venue best suited for dealing with environmental and economic discusses in the Arctic.

Arctic state members (coastal and non-coastal states) and Permanent Participants are not the only actors involved in daily diplomacy at the Arctic Council. Observer members also play a role, but the exact nature of this role, and how new members contribute to it, is less clear. Chapter 7 provides an analysis of the Arctic Council's management of the observer status. It looks at the increased interest in participation in the forum by non-Arctic states, IGOs, and NGOs to change the forum into a treaty-based organization, and the pressure under which the Arctic states and Permanent Participants find themselves to allow the observers a greater say in the forum's discussions and work.

The final chapter explores the challenges that Arctic states face in their effort to evolve the Arctic Council, specifically how to manage emerging regional issues that fall outside of the Arctic Council mandate. This chapter discusses how the Arctic states and Permanent Participants navigate these external pressures, while manoeuvring within their internal hierarchies. The aim of Part Two is to highlight how the Arctic states handle increased interest in the Arctic region and pressures for greater involvement on the part of non-Arctic actors like states and NGOs, to have a greater say in the region's governance. Again, as in Part One, this section focuses on challenges that were raised during my interviews in 2016 and 2017, but it is not meant to be an exhaustive list of the challenges faced by all representatives and the council as a whole.

The work and diplomacy within the Arctic Council will become increasingly important as the Arctic region emerges on the international stage as a hub for economic development opportunities and environmental risks. The Arctic Council has pioneered regional research and cooperation, but as the needs and pressures on the region grow, the forum faces challenges to its structure and norms. As a club structured around the Arctic states, with the support and close cooperation of the Arctic Indigenous peoples, the present format of the forum depends on this core group remaining united. The Ukraine conflict was a wake-up call, reminding the Arctic states, Permanent Participants, and their representatives about how vulnerable regional cooperation is and of the central importance of unity as the overarching empowering element to the Arctic Council. This book delves into the challenges of maintaining the club and its unity. It reveals the frank awareness of some of the representatives of the Arctic states and Permanent Participants that there are areas for improving regional cooperation. These representatives are diligently working to improve and evolve aspects of the club to prepare it, and those they represent, for the dawning of the new Arctic age.

1

Conceptualizing the Book

The politics governing the council's structure are influenced by many things: the systemic context of the time in which it was created, the status of its members in the international arena, and the history of the institutions and institution-building that preceded it. Acknowledging these influences allows us to more critically explore the factors driving and shaping the evolution of the Arctic Council, and the means by which its members identify and address its challenges.

A study of all the structures within which the work of the Arctic Council is conducted could be cumbersome. However, in order to understand how the Arctic Council operates and how its members identify and seek to address challenges, it is helpful to consider its forum as a club with defined parameters – a club concerned with the maintenance of its status. What allows us to think of the council as a club? One aspect is that through the Arctic Council the Arctic states pool a limited range of common resources on a case by case basis for their work such as environmental clean-up, and other initiatives for and within the Arctic region. They also bring together their collective authority and legitimacy as recognized sovereign Arctic states in order to speak and act on behalf of much of the Arctic region. In this, they work with and are supported by the Arctic's Indigenous peoples who have Permanent Participant status, in order to maintain the focus of Arctic dialogue and actions within their shared forum. They have also mutually set limits on what they are willing to consider within the club, as indicated by their clear decision not to discuss directly or consider pooling resources on any military related matters in the region.

In international politics such clubs are plentiful, as is club diplomacy, the art and practice of conducting negotiations among actors such as states, pan-state actors, and organizations through their representatives. Club diplomacy differs from other forms of diplomacy in the sense that it is carried out among a limited group of actors, through their representatives, within the confines of a group – a club – with exclusive voluntary membership.

The motives underpinning the formation and purpose of clubs determine their practices in international institutions and forums. The Arctic Council's practices of identifying and addressing internal and external challenges to its daily operations help us to understand the relationship between its club formats and its diplomacy dynamics. As easy as it is to criticize the Arctic Council's member states for forming a body with elite status within which they alone hold the ultimate power to make formal decisions, such clubs exist in many areas of international politics. Various forms of clubs in international politics include NATO, the G8, and ASEAN, to name a few (e.g., Badie 2012).

My intention here is not to evaluate club diplomacy normatively, but to use the concept of club diplomacy as a tool to demystify diplomacy within the Arctic Council, so as to help researchers and policymakers understand the forum and the way those working within it address challenges and achieve desirable outcomes. Other important concepts such as status hierarchies and pecking orders can shed light on the way actors such as the Arctic states and their representatives to the Arctic Council approach issues of regional cooperation and identify and develop solutions to internal and external challenges. The dynamics of Arctic cooperation are fascinating, but to appreciate the nuances of the social dynamics of diplomacy in the region, we need to have a fuller view of the daily experiences of actors within the diplomatic milieu. This chapter sets up the framework that informs the analysis of the internal and external challenges of the Arctic Council that follows.

STATUS AND THE ARCTIC COUNCIL

Attributing status is not a straightforward matter, but the pursuit of status is a constant theme in international politics. The Arctic region is no exception. Ambiguity over markers of status means that "practitioners are left to debate amongst themselves about how to attribute privileges in institutional settings" (Pouliot 2014, 194). Deborah Welsh Larson, T.V. Paul, and William C. Wohlforth, authors of the book chapter "Status and World Order" (Larson et al. 2014) and editors of *Status in World Politics* (Paul et al. 2014), write that the status of a given state is determined by "collective beliefs about [its] ranking on valued attributes (wealth, coercive capabilities, culture, demographic position, sociopolitical organization, and diplomatic clout)" (Larson et al. 2014, 7; parentheses in original). They go on to describe status as "a collective, subjective, and relative social relationship involving hierarchy and deference" (2014, 13). Further, in international relations, "status manifests itself in two distinct but related ways: as membership in a defined club of actors, and as relative standing within such a club" (2014, 7).

Within the political dynamics of diplomacy in the Arctic, there are at least three dimensions of status involving the Arctic Council: the international status of the Arctic Council; the status of individual Arctic states and Permanent Participants within the Arctic Council; and the relative standing of individual representatives within the Arctic Council.

The international status of the Arctic Council is relative in the sense that it is not in direct competition with another forum or institution as the primary regional cooperation body of the Arctic. Its pursuit of status on the world stage is based rather on the interests and collective aspirations of the Arctic states and peoples and their understanding that their interests in the region have more weight if they present a united front internationally. At the same time, Arctic scholar Douglas Nord argues, a possible challenge to the forum's status may arise from the inside – namely from the "Arctic Five" (A5) coastal states (Nord 2010; also see Dodds and Ingimundarson 2012). As an example, the Arctic coastal states (Canada, Denmark, Norway, Russia, and the United States) sometimes exclude the non-coastal states (Finland, Iceland, and Sweden) from discussions about Arctic maritime issues, preferring to work among themselves outside the Arctic Council, as they did in preparing the 2008 Ilulissat Declaration. While I present an alternative view, positing that value is potentially added to Arctic solidarity through using the collective voice of the A5 (chapter 8), the fact remains that this smaller group has been perceived as a potential challenger to the status of the Arctic Council as a whole.

For the Arctic states as a group, however, issues of regional status are seen in a more outward-looking manner. A leading concern is the possible emergence of alternatives to the Arctic Council, such as arrangements for bilateral and multilateral cooperation and other forums or legally binding agreements. These are seen to have the potential to detract from the ability of the Arctic Council to maintain its status, and by extension, the status of Arctic states both within the forum and in Arctic governance.

There are those outside the Arctic state club who would like a greater say in how the region is used. China is a prime case in point (State Council Information Office of the People's Republic of China 2018). Depending on the contextual and systemic conditions at any given time, non-Arctic state actors could challenge the premise of the Arctic Council, and even possibly create an alternative venue for regional dialogue and decision-making. Larson et al. define authority as "a *legitimate* right to command over other states," adding that "the exercise of authority depends on status, which makes the exercise of power legitimate" (2014, 15). The legitimacy of a challenge to Arctic state leadership and status in Arctic governance would affect perceptions of the Arctic states' authority in regional management. This challenge could in turn be detrimental to the Arctic Council and its status.

A prolonged loss of status for the Arctic Council could signal a loss of legitimacy for the club, and by extension, to the power of the Arctic states that control it. The circular status of relationships means that damage to either part of it would risk creating a power vacuum in Arctic stewardship, leading to instability and governance gaps in the region, or to the rise of a challenger. The risk associated with the rise of a challenger forum or treaty, from the general perspective of current Arctic Council members, is that they would be less likely to have as much status in such a forum or treaty. That being so, the continued existence of the Arctic Council is in the interests of current Arctic Council member states. Internally, the club members (including Permanent Participants), jockey for relative status within the Arctic Council, which affords members, and by extension their representative, opportunities to influence the club's work and the direction of its evolution.

Larson et al. further note that "status matters both for the status-seeker and the perceiver" (2014, 17). A benefit of higher status is that it "enhances collective self-esteem, derived from pride in one's membership and social identity" and that it "brings with it deference to a state's interests and concerns" (2014, 18). While technically all Arctic Council member states are equal in the consensus decision-making processes, the reality is that inequality is always present in clubs. International politics and status scholar Iver B. Neumann observe that in Arctic cooperation, great power states like the United States and Russia can "fall back on the use of force should other ways of ordering conflict fail, [while] other powers cannot" (Neumann 2011, 567).

As for the comparatively smaller states, which are Western and rich (Canada, Kingdom of Denmark, Finland, Iceland, Norway, and Sweden), since they do not have hard-power resources comparable to those of the great powers to fall back on, they engage more in systems-maintenance diplomacy (Neumann 2011, 563). Systems-maintenance diplomacy rests on the assumption typically made by small states that they will never be great powers, but they "take responsibility for international peace and stability ... beyond [their] fair share," effectively acting like great powers to a degree, without attempting to be one. The smaller states are, rather, "trying to narrow the 'status gap' with greater powers" and compete with other small states "for status with their peers for good-power status" (De Carvalho and Lie 2015, 68–9).

Within Arctic diplomacy, the United States and Russia are generally recognized as ranking toward the top of the internal hierarchy of the Arctic Council, for a few reasons: their broader standing in international politics (their status as great powers with nuclear power and permanent UN Security Council membership), their counterbalancing influence on one another in geopolitics, and, in the case of Russia, its position as the geographically largest Arctic state. Nevertheless, the status and participation of these two great-power states does not make the clubs in which they are involved puppets to their interests. As Neumann notes, good ideas "have a greater chance of being realized if they emanate from great/super powers" (Neumann 2011, 572), as can be seen with the Gorbachev's 1987 Murmansk Speech indicating Russia's openness to non-military Arctic cooperation (Åtland 2008a, 305–6), but "small states certainly have a role to play" (Neumann 2011, 572).

The overall status positions of the United States and Russia vary on a case-by-case basis, with the medium and smaller Arctic states often ranking higher than them on specific topic areas. Examples of such topics are: representing Indigenous interests (Canada and Permanent Participants); financially supporting Indigenous participation (Canada, Norway, and the Kingdom of Denmark); managing and supporting forum finances (Norway); and leadership in renewable energy (the Kingdom of Denmark, Finland, Sweden, and Iceland).

The relative standing of representatives also plays a role in working relationships in the Arctic Council and between the forum and outside actors. Representatives try to increase their standing within diplomatic relationships because for representatives, just as for states and clubs, "status increases the possibility of exercising power" and "higher-status individuals … have more *perceived* influence over the outcome than those of lower status" even if "these perceptions are not always accurate" (Larson et al. 2014, 14).

In the context of the Arctic Council, each state is represented by a delegation of at least one representative, and the relative standing of these representatives can feed back into the status of their state. A good example is the way chairpersons conduct themselves and are perceived by representatives and delegations. The position of the chair rotates among the Arctic states every two years, and the chairperson is appointed by the state holding the chair to represent that state during its term. Normally the chairperson is a diplomat or government minister with years of experience operating in diplomatic negotiations. As I discuss in chapter 4, chairpersons often receive more attention than typical representatives, given that, during their chairmanship, they represent themselves, their state, and the Arctic Council. Although the position of the chairperson formally elevates that person's status over that of other representatives, their informal status among their colleagues at the forum may be quite different. This discrepancy may in turn affect their ability to use their formal status position as chair to direct the work of the forum and influence change. Overall, representatives' capacity to represent their state is influenced by the relative status of that state, but it is also influenced by their own ability to navigate pecking orders, procedures, and norms.

In addition to representatives' affiliation with a specific state, many other factors affect their standing. Such factors include: who they represent; their level of experience at the task to which they are assigned (researcher, diplomat, civil servant, rights campaigner, for instance); their level of connectivity to networks within the diplomatic environment; their level of education (which can include informal training such as mentorship as well as post-secondary education); and the financial resources at their disposal (to cover the costs of to travel to meetings, socializing with the diplomatic peer group, receiving additional training and support, and completing the work they are assigned). As this book illustrates, particularly in Part One, the identification and management of the internal challenges of the Arctic Council are affected by the standing of permanent members and representatives and the opinions they voice at the Council, while at the same time the capacity of the representatives to do their work is also influenced by the ways in which states select, prepare, and support their delegates.

CLUB DIPLOMACY

The concept of club diplomacy can be traced back to the nineteenth century and the Concert of Europe. Originally constituted of Austria, Prussia, Russia, and Great Britain, this Quadruple Alliance is referred to as "the true ancestor of club diplomacy"

(Badie 2012, 14). Bertrand Badie further depicts this system of dispute resolution: "It was based on the principle of common deliberation and unanimous decision-making. Its members were bound by solidarity without challenging their sovereignty. However, those who were excluded de facto had to abide by its choices: the oligarchs were sovereign because they were powerful" (2012, 15). Jeffrey Winters and Benjamin Page also speak of the role of wealth in their work on oligarchies: ultimately the "possession of great wealth defines membership in an oligarchy, provides the means to exert oligarchic power and provides the incentives to use that power for the core political objective of wealth defense" (Winters and Page 2009, 732). But wealth does not necessarily mean financial wealth alone; wealth can also come in the form of natural resources and territory.

The earliest literature to explore the links between club construction and membership emerged in the field of economics. According to Todd Sandler, a club is "a voluntary group deriving mutual benefit from sharing one or more of the following: production costs, the members' characteristics, or a good characterized by excludable benefits" (Sandler 2013, 267; see also Buchanan 1965). The concepts of clubs and club goods originated in the work of economist James Buchanan and his seminal piece "An Economic Theory of Clubs," in which he calls clubs "consumption ownership-membership arrangements." Buchanan calls club theory "a theory of co-operative membership" (Buchanan 1965, 1), arguing that a club is "a member-owned institutional arrangement for the provision of a club good that is subject to some rivalry in the form of congestion" – congestion being "a detraction in a club good's quantity or quality from increased utilization by the sharers" (Sandler 2013, 266).

Club theory was developed to help close the gap that exists between conversations about private matters and discussions about pure public goods. Club theory argues that clubs (airports, hospitals, libraries, and theatres, for instance) are distinguishable from pure public goods (the air, for instance) and private goods (cars, and clothing, and the like). The theory rests on two basic

assumptions: first, that "the presence of crowding requires a restriction of group size, so that membership size in an endogenous vari-
able"; and second, that "*both* membership size and provision are
interdependent allocation decisions" (Sandler and Tschirhart
1997, 336). Since club membership is finite, "nonmembers of a
given club have two options: join another club providing the *same*
club good, or not join any club providing that club good" (Sandler
and Tschirhart 1997, 337).

According to Frederic Sterbenz and Todd Sandler, models based
on club theory include the assumption that "club members are …
drawn from a homogenous population in which all individuals possess identical tastes and endowments" (Sterbenz and Sandler 1992,
2). As such "prospective members [are] forced to participate in a lottery prior to the composition of the club being determined" (Sterbenz and Sandler 1992, 1; see also Hillman and Swan 1979; Hillman
and Swan 1983). While these assumptions are in some instances
true, there are also other means of obtaining club membership, particularly in diplomacy.

Clubs are not always composed of homogenous actors, although
they always have some homogenous trait or purpose around which
they cooperate, such as shared defence or economic interests
(NATO, the EU, for instance). Similarly, club members are not always
forced to participate in a lottery to gain admission. Ultimately, a
club can only be created if some actors take the initiative, and being
a club founder may allow a member to circumvent a membership
lottery. The position of founder also empowers a member with the
potential to influence the way future club membership is granted
and under what conditions new members are expected to operate.
Notably, in the research on clubs, one area where there is a gap is
in the implications of clubs' hierarchical or authority structures
(Sandler and Tschirhart 1997, 339–44).

Although the composition of the Arctic Council is not identical to
that of the Concert of Europe, and there are obvious differences in
hard- and soft-power capabilities among member states, time period,
as well as the mandates and agendas of the diverse groups, the concepts of club-style diplomacy and oligarchy are informative if we are
to understand the context within which Arctic diplomacy occurs.

Like Badie's examples of club diplomacy, and models similar to the Concert of Europe, NATO, and the G8, the Arctic Council is based on a consensus decision-making model. The Arctic Council is also constructed on the premise is that no Arctic state has to concede its claims in the region to be a member of the club, even when such claims might overlap. The resolution of claims disputes is seen as a matter to be dealt with bilaterally between affected group members. As a result, unresolved disputes, such as the disputed maritime boundary in the Beaufort Sea between Canada and the United States, or the ownership of Hans Island, which is claimed by both Canada and Denmark, remain issues that these states must address on a bilateral basis and are not discussed formally at Arctic Council meetings (e.g., Burke 2018; Carnaghan and Goody 2006).

Outsiders who want to participate as observers in the club's predefined areas of discussion must abide by conditions for access, even from the sidelines. The first three conditions for participation by outsiders, as outlined by the Arctic states, are that they:

- accept and support the objectives of the Arctic Council defined in the Ottawa declaration;
- recognize Arctic States' sovereignty, sovereign rights and jurisdiction in the Arctic;
- recognize that an extensive legal framework applies to the Arctic Ocean including, notably, the Law of the Sea (Arctic Council 2015c, 2015g).

If an applicant for observer status is not willing to abide by these stipulations, then that applicant is excluded. The Arctic states have exclusive control over access to the regional forum. Observer status, for example, can be revoked if a state, IGO, or NGO acts in a way that is perceived as contravening the terms to which they agreed in order to obtain observer status. Since it is a consensus body, only one of the eight Arctic states needs to withdraw its approval in order for an observer status to be revoked and for an observer to be ousted from the club. With the power to permit or deny club access, the Arctic states have cemented their hierarchical position over other actors.

Unlike some other clubs like the Concert of Europe and NATO, the Arctic Council is explicitly designed to exclude military issues and makes a point of avoiding discussions about military matters (Arctic Council 1996). This mandate is quite important, as it signals both that the club is not meant to be some sort of regional military alliance or discussion platform and that the forum lacks direct influence on hard-power issues in the region. The Arctic Council's narrow cooperation mandate as a club does not mean, however, that it lacks influence.

According to Rebecca Adler-Nissen and Vincent Pouliot, the "power baseline of pre-existing assets does not exhaust the variety of resources that structure power relations" (2014, 893). Rather, "some power resources are produced locally, in and through a particular practice" and "most performances of a practice contain an implicit claim of authority – that 'this is how things are done'" (Adler-Nissen and Pouliot 2014, 893; quotations in original text,). In other words, the acts of establishing and practising cooperation in a club like the Arctic Council can produce both local power resources such as legitimacy for certain types of actions and authority claims. An example of an authority claim is the argument that the Arctic Council is the pre-eminent Arctic cooperation body. The Arctic Council lacks agency, in the sense that anything discussed, funded, or agreed upon at the forum requires state approval and support. However, as it is often seen – and spoken of – as the pre-eminent forum for the region, the council does have a power that its core members cultivate, protect, and draw upon to influence perceptions of initiatives proposed for the Arctic.

While it is true that practitioners, in the course of performing their trade, stake a claim in how things are done, at the same time, "the structuring effects of practices are often not intended as such [but] are side effects" (Pouliot 2016a, 13). This unpredictability can in turn affect the power resources available to practitioners. Club members can find themselves navigating structures and norms, as well as pressures they may not have anticipated to encourage those structures and norms to evolve in certain directions. In some instances, club members and their representatives have to navigate constraints they thought they had avoided when they first established the club's format. As a consequence, the side effects of practices can lead to unanticipated strengths or challenges for clubs, which may frame the power resources at its disposal and the norms and structure of the environment within which diplomacy unfolds among club members and their representatives.

Ultimately, clubs rely on outside actors to help validate the status and power produced locally in and through club practices. This validation by others entails a difficult and continuous process of status-seeking – a tough process of finding a balance, because the practice of seeking status validation in turn shapes or influences how a club behaves. This balancing act is complicated by the fact that there are power imbalances among states and representatives within clubs (e.g., Pouliot 2016a, 6). Club members can differ in their views on the club's agenda and evolution, and on the degree to which outside actors can help with the achievement of this agenda, without undermining their club's status.

The power resources of the Arctic states generated through preparation for, and practices at, the Arctic Council include:

- language (both specific words and phrases, and types of languages spoken);
- consensus decision-making structure;
- financial contributions;
- selection and preparation of delegates;
- communication styles to various audiences;
- agenda-setting for meetings;
- process of admitting observers and parameters surrounding their participation.

Maintaining these power resources is steady work for the Arctic states, Permanent Participants, and their representatives. Systemic changes in the context within which these resources exist can present challenges for a club while its members also manoeuvre to maintain their individual status within the club and in Arctic politics more generally.

At the same time, clubs need to maintain and strengthen their power resources. In a club, the core membership can constitute an oligarchy and they are incentivized to act in a way that ensures their continued control of the club. The general perception of the Arctic states' reluctance to include observers and Permanent Participants as equals to them, for example, is a natural position for core club members at the Arctic Council to take. As Badie notes: "Within its internal structure, an oligarchy benefits from a process of reproduction. But as powerful and resistant as an oligarchy may be, it enjoys only limited institutional protection. It is thus at the mercy of social change, of the evolution in resources and parallel ascensions that can dispossess and renew it, following the well-known image of 'history as a graveyard for aristocracies'" (Badie 2012, 98, quotations in original text,).

Systemic changes in international and regional politics also mean that the social and political landscape in which the Arctic Council was negotiated and created (the late 1980s and early to mid-1990s) has shifted, and the Arctic states now have to respond to these changes. In the twenty plus years since the forum's creation, for example, Indigenous peoples have gained, and continue to gain, increasing autonomy at the national levels of the Arctic states, although the degree to which this is happening varies significantly from state to state (e.g., Josefsen 2010; Loukacheva 2009). This means that Indigenous peoples have more and more political and legal power that allows them to influence politics at the national level, and which in turn helps them exert influence at the international level as well. In July 2017, for example, Canada's Supreme Court made a landmark ruling that "quashed plans for seismic testing in Nunavut" for oil exploration by a Norwegian consortium, on the basis of inadequate consultation with Indigenous people in Clyde River by the National Energy Board (Supreme Court of Canada 2017; see also Tasker 2017). This ruling signalled the growing recognition of Indigenous peoples' rights and their need to be part of decision-making processes affecting their communities (Supreme Court of Canada 2017; see also Tasker 2017). The inclusion of Indigenous peoples in decisions involving the Arctic region represents a shift from a mindset whereby Indigenous involvement was invited out of courtesy (and sometimes optics), to one whereby it is deemed essential for the legitimacy and success of decisions.

The emergence of new global powers such as China and India, and the increase in international interest in the Arctic region, has also moved the Arctic into the limelight. Concerns over such things as the impact of climate change on the region, and the rising interest in emerging economic opportunities in the region, have changed the profile of the Arctic. At the same time as the Arctic's profile has increased, so too has the growing economic and political clout of Asian states in international politics (e.g., Nye 2011, 46; Charturvedi 2013; Jakobson 2010; Jakobson and Peng 2012; Stokke 2013). In addition, international discontent with the current legal framework protecting high seas around the world has also gained heightened attention, leading to discussions about Law of the Seas reforms (e.g., Gjerde et al. 2008; Koivurova and Molenaar 2010). As a result, the Arctic Council and its core club members have had to adapt to the changing international political landscape.

As a club, the Arctic Council is not unique in its reluctance to fully include new members. This reluctance is observable in other international clubs, the G8 being an example. When the G8 members (Canada, France, Germany, Italy, Japan, Russia, United Kingdom, and United States) opened up to the idea of the formation of the G20, they were reluctant and protective of their elevated status (Badie 2012). (Since the publication of Badie's book, the G8, which came into being when Russia joined the G7 in 1997, has again become the G7 as a result of Russia's expulsion in 2014 in the wake of the Ukraine conflict.) At that time the G8 members felt they could no longer resist the pressure to allow more voices into their club. Given the nature of club politics, it will come as no surprise that the new framework to which the G8 agreed was specifically crafted so that the existing members could maintain the exclusivity of their club. As Badie reflects: "Before the G20 was really born, the G8 had to protect its reputation at all costs and not allow the idea – finally being acknowledged – of a new world directorate to be subverted" (Badie 2012, 89). During the process, "Western governments knew that it was no longer possible to ignore the emerging powers, in particular Asia, but it would be detrimental [to their status] to admit them too quickly into the club on a totally equal footing" (Badie 2012, 90).

The G20 emerged because the G8 faced substantial loss of legitimacy as a result of the 2007–08 financial crisis. The financial crisis emphasized doubts about the G8's leadership in managing global financial affairs and its lack of representativeness (Gronau 2016, 108–9). The G8's opening of global financial affairs to the G20 was a strategic move. Rather than replace the G8, the G20 operates alongside it (Badie 2012). As the G20 is also an explicit club, it also serves to reinforce the value and validity of using a club format in international politics, and formal recognition of the G20 helps address the problem of lack of representativeness of which the G8 has long been accused.

The reality that clubs must deal with norm- and rule-breaking within their ranks leads to certain decision-making processes aimed at club preservation. Badie's work helps explain why clubs behave as they do, particularly when one of their group members is perceived as misbehaving. The concept of club diplomacy and status hierarchies, for example, helps us tunderstand how the 2014 Ukraine conflict was managed within the Arctic Council, and why Canada's divergence from the expectation to leave military conflict issues out of the forum was so poorly received (explored in greater detail in chapter 4) (e.g., Exner-Pirot 2016). A compelling explanation is that "in club-style diplomacy, the idea is to survive as an oligarch by covering the errors of one's fellows" (Badie 2012, 22).

At the time of the Ukraine conflict, Canada held the Arctic Council chairmanship and it used its position to repeatedly attack Russia's repatriation/annexation of the Crimea region (Russia and the other Arctic states disagree on how to describe Russia's actions against Ukraine). Canada's actions against Russia while the Arctic Council chair were targeted toward a domestic audience (Exner-Pirot 2016); Canada's stance on the Ukraine conflict in the Arctic Council was partially meant to help a weakening national government drum up nationalistic sentiment and political support going into a general election. But the Canadian government failed to account for the context in which the behaviour was being displayed. At the time, since Canada was serving as Arctic Council chair, it was meant to guide the forum through the difficult

Ukraine conflict period and ultimately safeguard the forum's unified position. Instead, under the leadership of Stephen Harper, Canada chose to act individualistically, thereby undermining the forum's unity and Canada's status in the internal pecking order.

The other Arctic states were more reticent than Canada about Russia's behaviour toward Ukraine, although they condemned it outside the forum (through the imposition of sanctions and expulsion of Russia from the G8, for example). A good explanation for the other Arctic states' approaches toward Russia during the Ukraine conflict is their unwillingness to follow Canada's example of criticizing Russia within in the Arctic Council; they opted instead on "connivance," a willingness to turn a blind eye to something for the sake of the continuation of diplomacy on an unrelated matter. As Badie articulates their stance: "The 'smaller nations' make use of the connivance that brings them together in diplomatic concerts; though they remain in principle attached to the ideal of equality among states, they remind us how unrealistic that is in a world where such states are too numerous, too divided, and considerably different in their capabilities" (Badie 2012, 101).

Without Russia, Arctic cooperation and the projection of regional unity cannot succeed. The fact that Soviet/Russian openness to regional cooperation was the catalyst for the original construction of the forum's present-day cooperation, structures, and practices illustrates Russia's key role in making regional cooperation truly a regional endeavour. Russia is the largest Arctic state, a key focus for many Arctic Council environmental clean-up projects over its over twenty-year history, and a space to work with Russia as a partner rather than an adversary. Were the Arctic Council to disintegrate, the smaller Arctic states would arguably have more to lose than the larger ones in terms of their status and their leverage in international politics and the diplomatic channels it affords. Smaller powers are therefore likely to be more motivated to use connivance within the region to overlook Russia's behaviours outside of it.

Overall, club diplomacy is prevalent throughout international politics. As a club, the Arctic Council's behaviours are affected by the nature of the club's structure and working dynamics, as well as by systemic changes in international politics. The political landscape within which the Arctic Council operates is evolving, and this changing landscape influences how challenges to the Council are identified and addressed. The political landscape now includes such factors as the emergence of key political players (such as China), changing levels of interest in the Arctic region and high seas governance, and the growing political and legal influence of Indigenous peoples in the Arctic states. None of these factors exist-ed (or existed to the same extent) when the club was formed, yet all of them buffet the forum, and press it to change.

MULTILATERAL DIPLOMACY AND PECKING ORDERS

In the scholarship of mainstream international relations there is a tendency to focus on the exceptional – exceptional diplomats or events (Pouliot 2016a, 7). Exceptional moments and leaders, like the Ukraine conflict and Vladimir Putin, capture our attention and can have a profound impact on domestic and international poli-tics, focusing scholarship on these exceptions. But they also over-shadow the seemingly mundane practices of daily life that contin-ue regardless of exceptions and which account more for the way things are perceived (Pouliot 2016b, 8); they provide us with in-complete narratives. At the same time, permanent representatives in multilateral diplomacy "are aware of a number of internal dynamics that escape the capitals' knowledge. As a partly secluded social configuration, multilateral diplomacy develops its own tem-porality" (Pouliot 2016a, 20; 2016b, 134). Everyday events and "seemingly anecdotal diplomatic practices actually play a funda-mental – if oft overlooked – role in making the world go round" (Pouliot and Cornut 2015, 298).

The dynamics of regional politics and cooperation in the Arctic reflect the existence of diplomatic pecking orders and status hier-archies, both within the Arctic Council club, and between club members and outside actors. As Pouliot describes them, pecking orders, are "the informal hierarchies of standing that pervade mul-tilateral organizations" which "emerge out of the multilateral diplomatic process itself" (Pouliot 2016b, 2). A state's position in a

pecking order, much like that of a delegate, is relative; it is determined in comparison to other actors.

"The overwhelming majority of multilateral diplomacy," Pouliot
reminds us, "is uneventful and mundane," and these daily practices, which make up the core of multilateral diplomacy, are
frequently undervalued in international relations scholarship
(Pouliot 2016b, 9). Dialogues and informal interactions among
diplomats are a neglected part of international relations studies.
Pouliot further argues that diplomacy is not a thin veneer or a
social lubricant to conceal pecking orders determined by structural features (Pouliot 2016b, 17), observing in addition that "the cultivation of standing … is a never-ending process" (2016b, 64). The
practice of diplomacy, including its mundane daily interactions, is
important, as it is the daily practices in diplomacy that shape interactions among states and enforce international pecking orders and
status hierarchies.

Diplomats are not blank slates. They represent national interests
and are themselves products of socialization processes that stem
from factors such as their backgrounds, formation and education,
and workplace experiences. At the same time, "people are not cultural dopes but actors in a social theater," and they too must be
considered when looking at decision-making processes (Pouliot
2016b, 54). Pouliot cautions that, while "one should not overesti-
mate the role played by state representatives," this does not mean
that representatives do not contribute (2016b, 83). Instead, he says,
their principal contribution is "reactive, in managing the consequences of the international pecking order on their country's
standing at the multilateral table" (2016b, 83).

In the case of the Arctic Council and the challenges it faces in a
changing world, representatives assigned to this forum have the
two-fold task: fulfilling the Council's mandate as interpreted by
their member-states and managing the forum's premier status as
the principal regional cooperation forum. A role on the frontline
of diplomacy provides a unique vantage point from which to
reflect on challenges to cooperation within the club. This vantage
point is particularly important because "ways of doing things are

socially meaningful, a trait that requires paying attention to sense making" (Pouliot and Cornut 2015, 302).

At the moment, the Arctic Council enjoys a recognized elevated status in international politics as the Arctic's premier regional cooperation forum. By extension, the eight core member-states are recognized and acknowledged collectively for their central role in regional governance and diplomacy. This international recognition is supported to the extent that the members can stay united and focused on specific actionable issues and interests that transcend borders (like pollution), while maintaining their sovereignty. States create a web of status and authority through clubs. This is exactly what the Arctic states and their representatives in the Arctic Council have been working to achieve: "The Arctic Council wants the perception to be [that] if you are going to discuss environmental protection in the Arctic ... the Arctic Council is the pre-eminent forum to do that. And of course, they have the credentials to prove that" (Permanent Participant representative, 24 May 2016).

Status is not static, and the Arctic Council does not have an assured standing in international politics. As one representative noted:

> There is an acknowledgement that there is always a chance that there is something which might usurp the Council authority in the area. That being said, I think that there is a real effort to make sure that the council keeps itself ahead of that. And so, an example of course is trying to stay ahead of this issue [like the one] with the observers and [their] rumbling that [since] our involvement here isn't getting anywhere then we're going to go somewhere else. (Permanent Participant representative, 24 May 2016)

Pouliot acknowledges that the "politics of recognition ... sets the bounds of the struggle for practical mastery" (Pouliot 2016b, 66). Similarly, as Margaret Karns and Karen Mingst put it, the diplomacy of coalition-building "involves negotiating a common position, then maintaining cohesion and preventing defections to rival coalitions" (Karns and Mingst 2013, 147, quoted in Pouliot 2016b, 140).

In the context of the Arctic, therefore, the need to maintain the status of the Arctic Council as well as the status and authority of the Arctic states, underpins any discussion of the pressures felt by the representatives and how both the forum and the states are being approached. The ways in which this is being achieved, however, reflect the fact that "emerging practices stem from existing practices" (Pouliot and Cornut 2015, 306). This is both a beneficial aspect of diplomatic practices and at times a drawback.

During the initial decade of its existence, the Arctic Council operated in relative isolation. As a result, the Arctic states and the Permanent Participants had the time to construct their club and learn how to develop effective diplomatic practices. They were also able to entrench themselves and their interests in the design of the forum, making sure that their agendas would dominate the forum's work. The aim of member-states is now to maintain the club's status. This requires them to navigate the internal hierarchies in such a way as to relatively satisfy its core members, at least to the extent that they prevent defection from the group, while also remaining an attractive forum for multilateral diplomacy that outside actors want to participate in and contribute to.

METHODOLOGY

The main form of primary data collection done for this book was semi-structured interviews, supplemented by research using the Arctic Council's website and digital open access archives. Initial interviewees were identified through official webpages (e.g., Arctic Council website and university websites) and through my professional network from earlier projects. After the initial interviews, the Arctic Council representative and diplomat interviewees were identified primarily through the snowball method – approaching people recommended by previous interviewees. A few additional interviewees were approached after recommendations from third parties met at conferences and during visiting scholar placements.

In total, 120 people were contacted for interviews, of whom 66 were interviewed.

I undertook this fieldwork in 2016 and 2017 throughout the Arctic countries. Of the 66 interviews I conducted, 7 were research design and advisory conversations. Of the remaining 59 interviews, 34 were conducted with Arctic state and Permanent Participant representatives to the Arctic Council and with diplomats; 4 with researchers based at think tanks; 10 with established international academics who write and research in fields related to the Arctic (political science, international relations, sociology, history, economics, and biology); 3 with high-ranking diplomats (e.g., former and current ambassadors and individuals with at least 25 years of experience in the foreign service) from Arctic countries; 2 with elected officials from Arctic countries; 5 with civil servants from various Arctic state ministries (such as defence, environment, and foreign affairs); and one with a representative from an NGO heavily involved in Arctic environmental campaigning.

Archival materials from the Arctic Council's open access repository also informs the scholarship of this book, especially helping to identify and trace changes in one of the forum's key issues – funding. The theoretical literature and sources that inform this analysis (outlined in the introduction) have had the effect of pushing the analysis of the internal and external challenges to the forum beyond a mere shopping list of challenges toward a broader discussion about club behaviours in international relations. This book is not intended to provide a complete list of the challenges to the Arctic Council. It is a focused piece that analyzes the key challenges the council faces, as identified by practitioners. On the basis of feedback from representatives to the forum, it highlights the council's key internal and external challenges, with the hope of encouraging discussions in current scholarship about challenges in Arctic cooperation to include a more explicit recognition of the influence that the forum's diplomatic dynamics have on the way these challenges are identified and addressed.

When I approached interviewees for this research, I promised that their names and any identifiable characteristics such as gender, permanent workplace, country of origin would not be disclosed during the publication and dissemination of research findings. Some prospective interviewees, particularly state representatives and diplomats, directly expressed concern about being identified. The diplomatic and research community in the Arctic Council and Arctic politics is relatively small. To reveal the identities of some interviewees who were comfortable with having their names associated with their comments and not others would risk exposing the identity of some participants. As a result, I have excluded all identities but have retained generic terms such as "former representative to the Arctic Council" instead.

The majority of the interviews directly referenced in the book are interviews with people who have represented their states or their peoples (Indigenous representatives); accordingly, such interviewees have been referred to as representatives and delegates in order to acknowledge their roles. Occasionally there is some specification, such as an indication as to whether the representative is or was a diplomat to a foreign embassy or consulate, or represented a Permanent Participant. This specification is given in order to highlight the views of Permanent Participant representatives in contrast to state representatives and to distinguish between reflections from diplomats, who have broader diplomatic experience, and representatives working on specific Arctic Council portfolios.

Some interviews reflected in this work are not directly quoted or explicitly referenced, as per the request of participants, but interviews with these individuals have nevertheless served as vital background for this book. These individuals offered literature suggestions, opportunities to discuss and debate preliminary analyses, recommendations for interviewees, and suggestions for project design. My fieldwork also involved interviews with diplomats who had been posted to Arctic states, most of whom had experience in the Soviet Union, Russia, Ukraine, and Eastern Europe. These interviews focused more explicitly on their opinions on cooperation among Arctic states in the Arctic region and on their views of the implications of the Crimea conflict on Western relations with Russia, the Russian government's motives in international and domestic politics, and Russia's national identity.

What differentiates this book from existing scholarship is its focus and approach. It uses the approach of conventional qualitative content analysis and draws on the literature on diplomacy and on practice theory to help inform the discussion and to give a richer account of the Arctic's regional cooperation dynamics than presently exists in international relationships scholarship.

Content analysis was used in the identification of the core challenges highlighted in this book; rather than use preconceived categories, "the categories and names for categories ... flow from the data" (Hsieh and Shannon 2005, 1279). Interviews were the primary source of data collection; with the exception of the research on funding, which was significantly supplemented by post-interview evaluation of archival materials found on the Arctic Council Open Access Repository. In the interviews, questions tended "to be open-ended or specific to the participant's comments rather than to a pre-existing theory" (Hsieh and Shannon 2005, 1279). Examples are: *What do you think are the key strengths of the Arctic Council? What do you think are the key challenges of the Arctic Council? Can you elaborate on why you believe these are the key strengths/challenges?*

Interview notes and transcripts were coded to highlight the core themes about the Arctic Council's daily work and the strengths and challenges of undertaking it, as reflected upon by interviewees. The book's core themes – internal versus external challenges – became the structuring framework for the empirical analysis. This was followed by the identification of secondary themes, which became the chapters in Part One and Part Two of the book – (internal) funding, institutional memory and knowledge depreciation, keeping national politics out of the forum, language barriers, (external) communication and misunderstandings, the observer question, and coastal *versus* non-coastal states and the pressure to evolve. Lastly, it became evident that within the secondary themes there were differences in how these challenges were conceptualized and discussed and what elements of the challenges stood out as the most important from the perceptions of the various interviewees. These variations became the tertiary level of analysis and make up the subsections within the chapters that address the differing emphases on the challenges.

THE RUSSIAN OUTLIER IN THE ARCTIC EQUATION

Within the Arctic Council, effort was made to prevent the Ukraine conflict from undermining the mutual willingness to work on shared agendas. The Western Arctic states have tried to isolate the daily interactions with Russia at the Arctic Council from their diplomatic relations with Russia in other political contexts. Their object is to safeguard two decades of successful network-building with Russian officials and government departments, and the shared Arctic agenda between them and the Western Arctic states. Keeping Arctic Council diplomacy isolated has proven difficult at times. Russia has made it clear, in international politics more generally, that it is willing and able to stand up and push back, hard, against disapproval from other states about the Crimea region (e.g., Retired diplomat, 9 May 2016; Retired diplomat, 11 May 2016). With the seven other Arctic states opposed to Russia's stance on Ukraine and the Crimea region, separating Russia's global ambitions from its Arctic ones has at time severely strained dialogue in the Arctic Council.

Many of the representatives and diplomats whom I spoke to reflect that Russia "is a civilization unto itself and should be regarded and respected as such … Russia is a proud old tough bear" (Retired diplomat, 9 May 2016). In the past few decades, Russia has suffered a number of major psychological hurts, including the collapse of the Soviet Union, ongoing economic struggles, and a decline in status within international politics (see Westdal 2016). Those working close with Russian representatives and diplomats reiterated that people in the West and their representatives need to broach discussions with Russia with a level of respectful acknowledgment of their different views and priorities in the Arctic (and elsewhere), and reminded those analyzing the actions to not skew respectful acknowledgement as equating to approval or support for actions or policies. To do otherwise would not serve the interests of regional cooperation, either with respect to international politics generally or to Arctic cooperation within the Arctic Council specifically.

The fact that successful engagement with Russia is needed for the Arctic Council to function was a point emphasized by delegates and diplomats. A former diplomat from an Arctic state to Russia, who served as a diplomat there before and after the fall of the Soviet Union, observed that for Russians: "The Arctic is bred in their bones. They think of themselves as a northern people with great expertise in the Arctic ... The Russians have more Arctic, more people there, and have been there longer" (Retired diplomat, 9 May 2016). This former diplomat elaborated, noting that "Russia was a more Arctic nation than the Soviet Union was [because], as the Soviet Union shrank into Russia, the Russians lost other sea access" (Ibid., 9 May 2016).

A Permanent Participant representative also observed that: "Russia has a very strong nationalistic feeling and very much sees itself as an Arctic nation, and Russia identifies with the exploration of the Arctic, with conquering the Arctic. I know there is a feeling for that in other places too, but in Russia it is a very strong feeling" (Permanent Participant representative, 24 May 2016). In addition to acknowledging Russia's strong sense of identification with the Arctic, there is also an acute belief among representatives that regional cooperation in the Arctic Council will not work without Russia – more so than for most of the other Arctic states, except for the United States. John English, Canadian academic and author of *Ice and Water: Politics, Peoples, and the Arctic Council*, reflected the existence of this dynamic even when the forum was being established. English acknowledges that "all Arctic states knew that the Russians and the Americans mattered most, each had an implicit veto of the proposed council" (English 2013, 226).

The comments of various representatives, both on and off the record, strongly indicated that keeping Russia at the table in the Arctic Council was an essential part of the forum's success. "What would happen to the Arctic Council if Russia left?" asked one representative. "It would collapse. It would absolutely collapse. Most of [the Arctic] is Russia, so how could you have an Arctic Council without Russia being there and participating in it? You have to the have the eight (Permanent Participant representative, 24 May 2016). Another representative commented similarly: "I think it's important, even though it does take some finesse, and may be comprising your goals, at least in the short term ... to keep the Russians in.

They are the biggest group. How can the Arctic Council work without it, if more than half of the Arctic leaves the organization? I don't think it can" (Permanent Participant representative, 25 May 2016).

The fact that relations between the Western Arctic states and Russia can sometimes be tense is not an original idea, but to use words like "annexation" and "illegal occupation" to describe the conflict between Ukraine and Russia over the Crimea region only serves to alienate a Russian audience who clearly have an alternative position on the issue. Since this book aims to explore challenges within Arctic Council cooperation, it is important to try and limit the implicit bias about motives that words "annexation" or "repatriation" imply for both sides. In an effort to acknowledge the dispute and tension but not to align this book or any interviewees with a specific side on the diplomatic debate, I refer to the dispute over the Crimea region as a "conflict" in this book.

PART ONE

Introduction to Internal Challenges

The Arctic Council is currently undergoing a number of internal challenges that the Arctic states are committed to trying to manage or address. The ways in which these day-to-day challenges are being tackled, and the extent to which they can be resolved, are influenced by factors that extend beyond the confines of the forum. Part One explores some of the key internal challenges to the forum. Using the literature highlighted in chapter 1, it illustrates that the internal dynamics of the Arctic Council offer a complex demonstration of diplomacy at work.

Vincent Pouliot states that in "everyday practices of diplomacy, practitioners operate in a relatively self-contained social environment, with its own ways of doing things that are only partly responsive to external dynamics" (Pouliot 2016b, 36–7). To a large extent, the Arctic states try to keep the Arctic Council isolated from external political dynamics, but this is not completely possible; nor is this segregation entirely productive in helping the forum respond to systemic changes in international politics. In additional, factors such as the relative size of the various Arctic states, in combination with their national relationships with the region, all play a role in the way challenges are identified, perceived, and approached by the forum's member-states at different points in time. In most cases, the influence of those factors can only be suggested rather than causally inferred with any degree of certainty.

International relations scholarship suggests, however, that "good ideas may have greater chance of being realized if they emanate from great powers" (Neumann 2011, 572). As a result, there are times when the proposer of ideas and the state with a relatively high pecking order placement in a certain topic and expertise area may be a smaller actor that happens to punch above its weight in a given area.

Part One illustrates that, when reflecting on the past and extent of the efforts to deal with the Arctic Council's challenges, it is important to remember, as Pouliot states, that: "Practices do change over time, although quite gradually. Pathbreaking deviations usually take root from the margins and accumulate over time" (Pouliot 2016b, 58). Correspondingly, Part One demonstrates that the systems maintenance of the Arctic Council and the current international political arrangements that acknowledge the Arctic states as central and dominating actors in regional governance, are primarily a focus of the small and medium power member-states. These states are more motivated to maintain order than the great powers (e.g., United States and Russia), who have greater means at their disposal to further their agendas (e.g., hard- and soft-power resources) and likely have less at stake if the initiative fails. Iver B. Neumann argues that for small (and medium) powers, there is a "general interest in institutionalization" and a preference for predictability, because "the more ordered and predictable the principles of conflict resolution are, the harder it is to convert military resources into influence over outcome" thereby neutralizing, to a degree, the relative advantage of great powers (Neumann 2011, 567).

Part One brings attention to the more prevalent internal challenges of the Arctic Council, as identified by those who work, or have worked, on Arctic Council diplomacy and diplomatic relations among the Arctic states. It explores the following issues: funding (chapter 2); institutional memory and knowledge depreciation (chapter 3); keeping national politics out of the forum and the role of the chair (chapter 4); and language barriers (chapter 5). These challenges were raised during my interviews with representatives to the Arctic Council, including past and present Senior Arctic Officials (SAOs), working group representatives, and chairpersons, in 2016 and 2017. Supporting information was

Table P1.1   Abbreviations for working group names

Abbreviations	Names of working groups
ACAP	Arctic Contaminants Action Program
AMAP	Arctic Monitoring and Assessment Programme
CAFF	Conservation of Arctic Flora and Fauna
EPPR	Emergency Prevention, Preparedness and Response
PAME	Protection of the Arctic Marine Environment
SDWG	Sustainable Development Working Group

Source: Arctic Council, 2015

obtained from interviews with diplomats and academics and from the Arctic Council's digital archives, in particular SAO reports and the 2001 Haavisto Report commissioned by the Arctic Council to review the structures of the forum (Haavisto 2001). My analysis aims to go beyond a simple outline of the challenges and seeks also to reflect the growing strengths of the Arctic Council, to acknowledge the work that has been done to address challenges, and to identify where further work may be required.

Table P1.1 outlines the working groups of the Arctic Council (Arctic Council, 2015), giving their short-form names, which will be used throughout the book.

This table will help the reader keep the various parts of the Arctic Council mentioned in Part One – namely the working groups – clear and avoid confusion with the abbreviations.

2

Funding

A major challenge that has far-reaching implications for the Arctic Council is the matter of its funding. A lack of transparency and understanding of the forum's finances risks its status and affects its ability to perform its required functions. The Arctic Council member-states recognize this problem and, particularly since the 2001 Haavisto Report, which reviewed the council's structures (Haavisto 2001), the forum has been working to address the financial details of its work.

The dynamics of the forum's current funding are indicative of its internal pecking orders. For the small and medium Arctic states, system maintenance has become a focus. Not only do they demonstrably contribute the greatest share of trackable funding to the Council's work but they are also the most eager to ensure that the forum continues operation. The states with higher status in international politics – the United States and Russia – appear on the surface to be less financially committed, although occasional examples contradict this observation. One instance is their contributions to the Project Support Instrument fund, discussed later in this chapter (Representative to the Arctic Council, 13 October 2016; see also Arctic Council Open Access Repository 2009).

The forum itself presently lacks a clear understanding of its finances, a situation that has persisted throughout its history. A full understanding of funding contributions by members is hampered by a lack of clear budgeting records and by the forum's diffuse fundraising processes. The ability to speak about contributions in detail is limited. As a result, my research relies on reflections of representatives and the slowly emerging financial details, which the Arctic Council discloses through its open access repository.

In the course of my fieldwork for this study, concerns related to funding were uppermost in the minds of interviewees and a subject of much nuanced discussion. The themes raised related to funding are broken into three sub-categories: determining how much the work of the Arctic Council costs; raising funds for separate aspects of the work within the forum; and the diffuse nature of the funding mechanisms that support Indigenous peoples and their participation in the forum. What became clear was that, where money is concerned, there is limited transparency. Only in recent years has the council begun to maintain consistent records of its finances. These efforts are necessary, as the council has reached the stage where greater financial accountability is needed in order to improve its efficiency and maintain its legitimacy. The overarching issue of funding remains the leading challenge to the forum's overall evolution and success.

DETERMINING THE COST OF THE ARCTIC COUNCIL

The absence of a clear picture of the forum's finances sends a negative signal to outside audiences about the Arctic states' management style. When the forum was relatively small and received little international attention, this was not a big issue. Since the mid-2000s, however, the Arctic and the Arctic Council have been scrutinized. The lack of financial clarity risks deterring observers from making financial contributions and offering support to the council. The Arctic states are well aware that this may be a problem, particularly as the forum expands to include more observers and attract more media attention.

In addition to finding new ways to involve observers and expand the forum's social media presence, the Arctic states are now making a greater effort to encourage observers to commit to the forum by increased participation in research and projects, and through financial support for the forum's work and the participation of the Permanent Participants. Financial transparency has therefore grown in importance. As a result, the Arctic states have begun to unravel the tangled web of budgets and contributions, and to look into alternative means of adding to the Council's budget. As one representative stated, "All the issues that the Arctic Council need to work on come back to funding" (Consultant to the Arctic Council, 14 June 2016).

In the process of sorting out the forum's finances, the greater inclusion of observers makes the Arctic states and Permanent Participants more susceptible to scrutiny from other actors. This is not necessarily a drawback for the Arctic Council, as greater scrutiny can inspire new ideas and avenues to broaden the impact of its work. Such scrutiny may also encourage greater efficiency, freeing up additional resources for projects. The fact that the Arctic states are now trying to sort out the Council's budget signals that they realize they must be more vigilant in their management style and accountability.

Many factors have contributed to the forum's lack of firm budget and accounting practices. When the Arctic Council was formed, the Arctic states decided that the council would not have a budget of its own. The United States' position at the time was reportedly that "financing and the notion of 'common costs' … should be abandoned" (English 2013, 231). Since the United States' involvement in the forum was perceived as crucial if the forum was to successfully engage Russia, the other Arctic states backed away from the budget issue. As a result, when it began to work in the 1990s, the forum had no concrete financial plan.

Nevertheless, funding did flow into the work of the Arctic Council through various channels. A combination of direct and in-kind financial support is used to fund the work of the Arctic Council working groups and the task forces (Arctic Council Senior Arctic Officials (SAO) plenary meeting 2016). Direct sources of funds, such as lump sums of money, are relatively easy to track and account for, as evidenced in the Arctic Council Secretariat's budget. In-kind support, also a popular form of funding received by the Arctic Council, is more difficult to track and determine its budgetary value. Examples include such non-monetary items as access to satellite imagery, labs, use of ships, researchers' salaries and other expenses, educational opportunities for the Permanent Participant representatives, and the provision of locations for meetings. These contributions have monetary value, but the value is not easily calculated into a dollar amount. Estimating the value of in-kind support adds a major layer of complexity to determining the actual cost of running the forum.

While funding may seem straightforward on the surface, the Arctic Council's finances are highly complex (Exner-Pirot 2016a). The most transparent part of the council's budget is that of the Arctic Council Secretariat (ACS), which was established in 2013 (discussed further in chapter 3). According to its 2015 Annual Report, the secretariat's budget for that year was USD $1,195,061, made up of equal lump sum contributions of USD $99,312 from each Arctic state. Norway, which is the host country for the ACS, contributed an additional $587,233 (Arctic Council Secretariat 2015, 38).[1]

When we look at factors that contribute to internal pecking orders and explore how and where certain states exert influence on the forum's evolution, Norway's role in Arctic Council finances stands out. To give a clearer sense of just how much financial support Norway has given the Arctic Council, in terms of proportion, notes from the plenary meeting of Senior Arctic Officials (SAO) Fairbanks meeting in 16–17 March 2016 record that: "The ACS is funded largely by the government of host country Norway, which contributes 42.5% of its budget each year. The remaining 57.5% of the annual budget is contributed equally by the eight Arctic states" (Arctic Council SAO plenary meeting 2016, 1). As the host country, Norway therefore contributes 42.5% of the budget of the ACS plus an additional (approximately) 7.2% as an Arctic state, for a total of 49.7% of the ACS budget. This proportion does not include other funding that Norway provides directly or through in-kind support for specific working group and task force projects, and to the Indigenous Peoples' Secretariat (IPS). Norway hosts and contributes approximately 50% of the IPS budget, with the Kingdom of Denmark contributing the other 50% (Permanent Participant representative, 24 May 2016).

Conventional international relations arguments about hierarchies in international politics focus primarily on structural features – material capabilities. Pouliot, however, points out that "multilateral diplomacy adds much more social complexity to stratification dynamics than what the generic structural model is able to capture" (2016a, 7). Norway's material capabilities in terms of wealth cannot in themselves account for its status as one of the most influential states in the Arctic Council. While Norway certainly does not fund all the Arctic Council's work, its reputation within the forum's diplomatic environment marks it as an indisputably integral part of the Council's success. The country's willingness to provide so much financial support, coupled with its good relationship with Russia and its skill in helping to keep Russia involved in the forum, are frequently noted by representatives from the other Arctic states (e.g., Retired diplomat, 9 May 2016; Retired diplomat, 11 May 2016; Consultant to the Arctic Council, 14 June 2016; Representative to the Arctic Council, 15 November 2016; Representative to the Arctic Council, 1 November 2017). Permanent Participants and representatives from the other member-states also acknowledge that Norway has achieved an elevated place within the forum's ranks. Due to the lack of transparency concerning the Council's overall operating costs and budget, it is challenging to clarify the relationship between Norway's financial support and its status within the forum.

As the Arctic Council has grown over the past twenty years, its budget has become increasingly complicated. A brief examination of the funding of the Council's working groups offers the best illustration of its budgetary complexity. The mandates of the six working groups are as follows:

- The Arctic Contaminants Action Program (ACAP): to "prevent adverse effects from, reduce, and ultimately eliminate pollution of the Arctic environment" (Arctic Council 2015b);
- The Arctic Monitoring and Assessment Programme (AMAP): to provide "reliable and sufficient information on the status of, and threats to, the Arctic environment, and … scientific advice on actions to be taken in order to support Arctic governments

in their efforts to take remedial and preventive actions relating to contaminants" (Arctic Council 2015d);

- Conservation of Arctic Flora and Fauna (CAFF): to foster cooperation "on species and habitat management and utilization, to share information on management techniques and regulatory regimes, and to facilitate more knowledgeable decision-making" (Arctic Council 2015e);
- Emergency Prevention, Preparedness and Response (EPPR): "the prevention, preparedness and response to environmental and other emergencies, accidents, and Search and Rescue (SAR)" (Arctic Council 2015f);
- Protection of the Arctic Marine Environment (PAME): "policy and non-emergency pollution prevention and central measures related to the protection of the Arctic marine environment from both land and sea-based activities" (Arctic Council 2015i);
- Sustainable Development Working Group (SDWG): proposing and adopting steps "to advance sustainable development in the Arctic"; "to protect and enhance the environment and the economic, culture and health of Indigenous Peoples and Arctic communities"; "to improve the environmental, economic and social conditions of Arctic communities as a whole" (Arctic Council 2015j).

The working groups are heralded as the workhorses of the forum. As these mandates illustrate, they have expansive objectives and previews. The working group budgets, however, are hard to decipher, given that they are funded through both direct and in-kind sources, and each one maintains its own budget.

The most accessible places to start efforts to understand the funding of the working groups are the six working group secretariats (WGS). Through them we can get an approximation of contributions to the working groups. Even these snapshots, however, only provide a narrow picture that does not reveal the particulars of expenditures on specific projects, or exact dollar figures for contributions; nor does it reveal how much the non-Arctic states and the other observers contribute to the working group budgets.

To start, the ACAP WGS and EPPR WGS are both part of the ACS and are funded as part of the larger ACS budget (Arctic Council Open Access Repository, Arctic Council 2016, 2–3). The AMAP WGS, however, is supported primarily by the Norwegian government, through funding that is in addition to Norway's other financial contributions to the Council (Arctic Council Open Access Repository 2016, 2). CAFF is funded by all the Arctic states, but figures on the distribution of these contributions, or their amounts, are not available to outside audiences at this time (Arctic Council Open Access Repository 2016, 2). The PAME WGS receives its primary support from Iceland (40–50%), with additional contributions from Denmark, Sweden, USA, Canada, and Finland; but, again, specific amounts are not available (Arctic Council Open Access Repository 2016, 3). Lastly, the SDWG WGS is funded mainly by Canada, with some support from Finland (Arctic Council Open Access Repository 2016, 3). The tendency appears to be that the smaller Arctic powers such as Norway, Canada, Iceland, and Finland contribute the bulk of the WGS budgets.

Estimating how much the administration and work of the working groups cost is not the Arctic Council's only challenge in determining its approximate budget. It is next to impossible to estimate the cost of the personnel who do the Arctic Council's work. Although the core of the manpower for the working groups and the task forces is made up of representatives from the Arctic states and Permanent Participant delegations, they are sometimes supported by observers as well as by individual scientists and consultants who are invited from around the world to contribute on a case-by-case basis.

State representatives in particular are often civil servants from a range of government departments, and sometimes scientific or legal experts, many of whom have national responsibilities beyond their work on Arctic Council issues. The salaries and budgets of these individuals are therefore often covered, to varying extents, by ministerial budgets, research grants, and other sources external to the Arctic Council. As a result, it is very difficult to calculate the cost of employing the people who go to the Arctic Council, and to determine what proportion of their work is devoted to Arctic Council–related activities.

Except for personnel at the ACS, participants in the Arctic Council are paid not from the Council budget but from other sources such as national and organizational budgets; even the IPS has its own budget. The work of civil servants on Arctic Council projects and research is not necessarily the sole, or even the principal focus of their job. How does one quantify the percentage of their salary that covers their work on council-related business? This is even further complicated by the confidential nature of a significant amount of information concerning salaries.

Adding to the confusion is the fact that a lot of the scientific research that is later used in Arctic Council reports is conducted by academics and experts, not by representatives.

> When you start looking into the people who are working on the different projects, it could be hundreds … And when you compare someone from Russia who is working for a monthly salary of 200 euros [with] a Canadian or Norwegian and try to put these together? In addition, what if you're using remote sensor data? How much is the contribution from the EU to provide satellite data? That's in billions a year and how much of that is going for the Arctic? (Representative to the Arctic Council, 13 October 2016)

While manpower is only one element of the range of factors that need to be considered in calculating the cost of the forum's work, difficulties with calculating staff/representative salaries or research budgets illustrate just how hard it is to construct a firm outline of the Council's past and current expenditures.

The lack of clarity about the Arctic Council's budget means that the Arctic states do not know exactly what resources they have available or at their disposal and how and where they are being used. The absence of this knowledge makes planning for the forum's future difficult. It is hard to make efficient use of resources that the forum has and to identify gaps where more are needed. The Arctic Council therefore faces a serious challenge when it comes to budgeting.

On 25 January 2016, the Arctic Council SAO chair (during the United States' chairmanship) asked the ACS to compile a general

overview of funding sources for the Arctic Council. The secretariat accomplished this task "in large part on input ... received from
the Working Group Chairs and Executive Secretaries ... and [this]
represents a first attempt to provide some insight into the main
funding streams" of the forum (Arctic Council SAO plenary meeting 2016, 1). As the Arctic Council funding overview document
from 2016 indicates (Arctic Council Open Access Repository
2016), and as people interviewed for this project all suggest, without the central role that Norway plays in the finances of the Arctic
Council's day-to-day management, the forum would not be able to
properly operate.

Having financial capabilities, however, does not necessarily
guarantee status. The practice of using those capabilities to
advance Arctic cooperation is nevertheless significant for gauging
Norway's relative standing, for example, within the Arctic Council's pecking orders. A number of interviewees noted that Norway
is known for being more willing to fund projects and ideas than
the other Arctic states. This willingness has arguably given Norway a more influential spot at the table in the Arctic Council, and
as a result, Norway is now more strategic in how it disburses its
support (e.g., Permanent Participant representative, 24 May 2016;
Consultant to the Arctic Council, 14 June 2016; Representative to
the Arctic Council, 19 May 2017). Norway has been able to successfully maintain its position as ACS host through its ongoing
financial commitment, along with its position as a solid partner
with Western states and its decades-long constructive engagement
with Russia.

In a sense, Norway has linked its status to its financial support,
such that its status would likely be negatively affected if it were to
reduce its support.[2] One former representative reflected on working with Norway to address environmental issues in the Russian
Arctic: "Often the Norwegians put a lot of money into that project
to incentivize everybody to work on this issue because it is in Norway's interest" (Former representative to the Arctic Council, 11
May 2016). Another representative interviewed in 2016 went into
greater depth about Norway's status but declined acknowledgment for their comments. This individual reflected that while Nor-

way does not like to be reduced to its pocket book, to the extent that it is, it is partly Norway's own fault, given that it has made a point of being front and centre in all funding discussions and is openly acknowledged for its contributions in any documentation available which mentions the budgets of the Arctic Council, the Arctic Council Secretariat, the working groups, and the Indigenous Peoples Secretariat.

The Norwegian practice of funding a significant portion of the Arctic Council's work is part of the social fabric of the dynamics of Arctic states' cooperation within the forum and is an important source of influence for Norway (e.g., Cox and Jacobson 1973, 410, in Pouliot 2016b, 45). The practice of routinely funding the Arctic Council, as much as the funding itself, is illustrative of Norway's concerted effort to establish itself as a broker in regional cooperation. According to Pouliot: "Brokers occupy central positions in networks thanks to stronger than average connections with more than one cluster ... Brokering renders others dependent on the broker for their interactions, both inside the cluster and between the clusters" (Pouliot 2016a, 23). As will come up later in this book (chapter 5), Norway's willingness to fund proposals gives it influence, and makes it a valuable ally to parties that are trying to forward ideas within the consensus decision-making dynamics of the forum's diplomacy. This is exemplified by the initiative to create the ACS to address institutional memory issues (see chapter 3).

When it comes to finding more specific budgetary information about the Arctic Council, however, hurdles remain. As one representative reflected on the challenge of deciphering the forum's budget: "The SAOs are constantly asking the same thing [budgets for the working groups] and it's really painful. Most of the work that is done is done by in-kind contribution. When [a working group] is writing an assessment, the countries are putting in the resources for that and ... it's impossible to evaluate it [the value of in-kind contribution] afterwards" (Representative to the Arctic Council, 13 October 2016). There is positive news, however, for budgetary reform and improvement in financial streams for the forum. The Project Support Instrument (PSI) is one of the strongest

Table 2.1
Financial contributions during PSI Pilot Phase 2009–2011

Contributor	Euros (€)
Finland	200,000
Iceland	8,000
Norway	237,700
Russian Federation	2,000,000
Sweden	272,000
NEFCO	450,000
Saami Council	12,000

Source: Arctic Council Open Access Repository, 2009

examples of new possibilities in attempts to help facilitate quicker funding mechanisms for the working groups.

RAISING FUNDS

The Project Support Instrument was introduced as a pilot program approved by the SAO on 7 April 2005, and it entered into a three-year pilot phase in 2009–11. The PSI is "a circumpolar funding mechanism for projects and actions related to prevention, abatement and elimination of pollutants harming the Arctic" (Arctic Council Open Access Repository 2009). As of 2009, about €12 million had been pledged to the fund, including a €10 million pledge from Russia. One representative noted that since that time the United States has pledged to contribute USD $5 million (Representative to the Arctic Council, 13 October 2016).

The fund manager for the project is the Nordic Environment Finance Corporation (NEFCO), which was established by the five Nordic countries (Denmark, Finland, Iceland, Norway, and Sweden) and is currently an observer in the Arctic Council. The funding allocated for the pilot phase totalled €2.46 million (Arctic Council Open Access Repository 2009). Table 2.1 gives a breakdown of the contributions for the 2009–11 pilot phase.

Although the PSI does not have a lot of money to allocate for projects and will not be a major game-changer for funding the forum's work at this time, it demonstrates an effort on the part of the Arctic states to find ways to fund work that is time sensitive, and an effort to work with observers and Permanent Participants to address funding challenges.[3]

The efforts to establish the PSI and the commitment of the United States and Russia have been helpful in developing the initiative. At the same time the involvement of these countries signalled their influence in the forum. One representative noted that "from the very beginning it was understood that the fund would not become operational until Russia put in its amount" (Representative to the Arctic Council, 13 October 2016). Russia held back on transferring its committed amount but did send it after the 2014 Ukraine conflict and the ensuing sanctions that were imposed. This surprised many in the Arctic Council. Russia's willingness to commit such a large sum of money may in part have been encouraged by the fact that "most of the PSI projects, in the near term, are expected to be executed in the Russian Federation" (Arctic Council Open Access Repository 2009). Russia benefits from the fund's work, given that the international sanctions that were imposed after the Ukraine conflict do not affect the Arctic Council's environmental work in Russia (Representative to the Arctic Council, 13 October 2016).

Funding a pilot project such as the PSI requires diplomatic skill and experience on the part of representatives, sometimes even more than the soundness of a proposal itself. Representatives have observed that the skill of representatives and the level of background knowledge they possess about their own country's funding mechanisms are very instrumental in pushing forward agendas and raising the financial capital needed to support projects.

For instance, when the Task Force on Arctic Marine Oil Pollution Prevention (TFOPP) was discussing the possibility of creating a legally binding agreement to address oil pollution preparedness and response (for more information on TFOPP see Arctic Council 2015k), Russia at first held back. But it skillfully navigated the situation:

Russia was at first reluctant to discuss binding agreements. But fast forward six months in the Task Force meetings, and all of a sudden Russia is talking about a binding agreement. And they were talking, "we really think this deserves a binding agreement amongst the Arctic states," and we were all looking at each other and wondering what had happened. There was all this speculation about where this had come from and a couple of things emerged. One was that Russia wanted to check this off their list and, if there was a binding agreement, they could point to it and say, "That's been dealt with; we don't have to go there again." The other reason is … that, if a binding agreement were signed within the ministry [of natural resources and the environment], a binding agreement jumps to the top of heap for funding … So within the team that was working on this, they knew [that] if they could get a binding agreement passed, they wouldn't have problems getting funding for the activities related to the agreement, because of the nature of the way [their] funding works. (Permanent Participant representative, 24 May 2016)

This observation of the Russian delegation within TFOPP reflects that, when it comes to making or suggesting projects and agreements, the skills of representatives and teams can be a deciding factor.

These skills, in combination with representatives' standing in the forum and nationally, have also played key roles in some close-call situations. Representatives can play an essential role in connecting the dots between ideas and funding when they have the expertise, status and window of opportunity to make things happen.

While the Russian representatives observed in the TFOPP negotiations showed ingenuity in practising their skill as diplomats and demonstrating Russia's status within the forum, the Permanent Participant representatives also play a key role in the diplomacy and negotiations. Unlike the Arctic states, however, the Permanent Participants face greater funding challenges with far-reaching implications.

FUNDING AND THE PERMANENT PARTICIPANTS

As can be seen with NEFCO's commitment to the PSI, a growing number of contributions (both financial and in-kind) are coming from observers to assist with the work of the working groups (Arctic Council 2017a; Arctic Council 2017b). An example of such support is Singapore's support of education opportunities for Permanent Participants, which aims to help build the organizational capacity of Permanent Participants (Burke and Saramago 2018). According to Singapore's ministry of foreign affairs, the cooperation package is meant to "share Singapore's experiences in areas such as maritime management with representatives from the AC PPs [Arctic Council Permanent Participants] through study visits to Singapore and also through technical courses and training" (Ministry of Foreign Affairs Singapore 2017). After becoming an observer in 2013, Singapore established the "Singapore-AC Permanent Participants Cooperation Package," which is "a customized technical cooperation package designed to enhance the human resource development and governance capacity of the [Permanent Participants]" (Arctic Council, Observer Report 2016).

The Permanent Participants have significantly fewer resources, compared to states, for developing their abilities to operate in international diplomacy. An offer such as Singapore's is a valuable option for Permanent Participants, as it gives them options to grow as organizations and increase their capacity. Permanent Participants have been taking advantage of this program. Four Arctic Athabaskan Council representatives, for example, used this program to take a course in Singapore on the impacts of climate change and adaptation strategies, and a Russian Association of Indigenous Peoples of the North (RAIPON) representative used the program to obtain a Master's degree in Public Policy (Arctic Council Observer Report 2016).

At the same time, however, long-term benefits accrue to Singapore as a result of Permanent Participants taking advantage of their offer of free education for their members. The promotion of an education program is a form of cultural diplomacy "designed to strengthen ties" (Lee 2015, 354) and a reflection of Singapore's eagerness "to forge new ties that accrue influence in a knowledge economy" (Lee 2015, 369). Singapore benefits in that those who participate in the educational programs it offers or supports are more likely to develop a positive perspective of Singapore, thereby increasing the likelihood of their giving Singapore favourable consideration in the future. Education is not benign. After all:

> Having former students in power positions in the public and
> private sectors back in their home countries, contextualizing
> and diffusing the knowledge learned in their foreign education,
> is an extremely valuable tool. It is not education alone ... but
> the education experience as a whole, which also generally
> includes many students coming to live and immerse themselves
> in the foreign country's society, learning and being exposed to
> its values, beliefs, and ideas. (Burke and Saramago 2018, 928)

Through the promotion of Singaporean culture via education, the state "can project a positive image, generate interest, promote exchanges, and engender trust for enduring partnerships" (Lee 2015, 354). By providing education opportunities via the Singapore-AC Permanent Participants Cooperation Package, Singapore is investing in the long-term benefits of education as a means of gaining influence in the Arctic Council. "Through this connection, international students develop meaningful relationships with the host country" (Lee 2015, 357). Ideally, these students would then promote ties between their home country and the host country.

Many states have used the approach of education to cultivate a greater appreciation of their values and institutions, hoping thereby to increase their capacity to influence the forum. Other examples are China, with the Confucius Institutes (e.g., Pong and Feng 2017); Confucius Institute Headquarters (Hanban 2014), and the United Kingdom, with Commonwealth Scholarships (e.g., Hart 2017). In Singapore's case, representatives from the Permanent Participants who are favourably disposed toward Singapore could be more likely to support suggestions for projects made by Singapore. This is a particularly useful tool for Singapore, because as an observer, its ability to propose and fund projects is restricted. Due to rules that restrict observers to contributing no more than 50 per cent of any given project, Singapore must have an Arctic state agree with any project proposal it puts forward, and support 50 per cent of that project (Arctic Council 2015c).

From the perspective of a Permanent Participant, or a member of their organizations, education is a costly and valuable commodity. For an actor trying to operate at the same level as nation-states in the Arctic Council but with considerably fewer resources, this is an attractive offer, one that comes with the promise of greatly increasing the capacity of the Permanent Participant.

The extent to which non-Arctic actors can contribute to the forum comes with a number of conditions, however. The Arctic states are aware that growing international interest in the Arctic could help them fulfil the Arctic Council's mandate. Increased interest gives the Arctic states a greater number of avenues through which they can solicit financial, intellectual, and material resources. As a result, observers are now being encouraged to play a larger role in the work of the forum.

While observer members are being called upon to contribute to the forum and the work and participation of the Indigenous organizations (e.g., through in-kind support such as Singapore's education package), contributions by observer members to the specific work of the working groups and task forces are more tightly controlled. Contributions are restricted in order to limit the extent that outside actors can influence the forum through their financial contributions. Council rules state that: "Observers may propose projects through an Arctic State or a Permanent Participant but financial contributions from observers to any given project may not exceed the financing from Arctic States, unless otherwise decided by the SAOs" (Arctic Council 2015g).

This restriction ensures that the Arctic states always remain in creative control of the direction of the forum's work. Even Permanent Participants are prohibited from independently funding a complete project. In this way, the eight member-states have woven themselves into the very fabric of the funding procedures, so that nothing advances without their involvement.

In comparison to the Arctic states, however, Permanent Participant organizations have far greater budgetary limitations. Permanent Participants have numerous funding arrangements with governments of the Arctic states and existing funding bodies like the IPS, which also help fund their participation in the Arctic Council.

The funding mechanisms and sources for the Permanent Participants are far from straightforward. For one thing, Permanent Participants have offices in several Arctic countries (with RAIPON being
the exception) and rely on various funding streams that do not necessarily apply to all branches of the umbrella organizations that
hold the Permanent Participant seats. Permanent Participants must
therefore be extra vigilant in obtaining and coordinating their
finances, because their organizations must be present at meetings
but travel in the Arctic is expensive. The need to be present at all
meetings is a major financial strain on the Permanent Participants,
as their absence from meetings means that decisions may be made
without them.[4]

Even though Permanent Participants are expected to operate at
a comparable capacity and level as the states, they lack the resources that formal state delegations to the Arctic Council have at
their disposal. David P. Stone, author of *The Changing Arctic Environment*, describes their difficulty:

> Although the permanent participant organisations receive
> funding to attend meetings of the Arctic Council and are pro-
> vided with a secretariat now located in Tromsø (Norway),
> there is no blanket funding to support their active participa-
> tion in Arctic Council projects or programmes. In some cases,
> a national programme … may provide some project funding
> or the working group secretariat may be able to organise
> funding. Otherwise, significant funding for participation in
> actual Arctic Council work tends to occur only when one or
> more of the permanent participants can carry out a compo-
> nent of that work. (Stone 2015, 30)

In the end, states have a preference for direct financial relationships with the branches of the Permanent Participant organizations that represents Indigenous peoples within their own state
(Gamble 2015, 4). Permanent Participants have their own
budgetary complexities because they tend to be unevenly funded and, as a result of there being different national branches
of the Permanent Participant organizations, have different funding streams.

CONCLUSION

The effort on the part of Arctic states to investigate the current operational costs of the Arctic Council and to formulate a financial plan going forward is not easily accomplished but, if the Arctic states are to maintain the status of the Arctic Council in regional decision-making and international politics, it is an essential one. Observers are now being asked to follow the lead of Arctic states in the forum and contribute financially – directly and in-kind – to the work of the council. As part of this policy, representatives have noted that the working groups, for example, are now taking note of which observers participate in their work – documenting commitment to the Arctic Council's work to help differentiate between those rhetorically expressing interest in the Arctic, and those actually committed to addressing issues in the region (e.g., Representative to the Arctic Council, 8 September 2017; Representative to the Arctic Council, 1 November 2017).

All these efforts are being made because the Arctic states are aware that the forum's current inability to account for its operating costs makes it vulnerable to challenges to its status and legitimacy. Challenges to the status of the Council itself could also raise doubts about hegemony of the Arctic states within the forum. Without a clearer sense of the forum's operating costs and contribution levels, it will likely become difficult to inspire observers to contribute, as the Arctic Council will have a difficult time demonstrating "value for money."

The present funding procedures and book-keeping practices may have worked when the forum was starting out, but as the forum grows, the current system is a source of trouble. The United States, for instance, may have had the ability to hold back the development of the forum's budgetary structures in the 1990s, but as the regional body becomes more prominent in international relations, resistance to at least accounting for the forum's expenses no longer seems a productive approach. Regardless, a full-fledged budget, with regular contributions from the Arctic states, is unlikely to become part of a new system for the forum at the moment, as it would move the forum away from the direct control of the Arctic states and empower possible independent decision-making in matters related to the forum itself.

Instead, a move toward greater transparency appears to be more realistic. A shift of this nature requires careful attention because, as we have seen in the case of Norway and Singapore, the supply of money can cultivate influence, which could inevitably have an impact the ongoing evolution of the Arctic Council, its internal hierarchies, and other dynamics, and could do so in unpredictable or undesirable ways.

NOTES

1   In addition to the sums contributed, the document also notes that fluctuation in the rate of currency exchange accounted for losses of USD $214,694, and the contributions deposited in 2014 added USD $15,776, as did the internal fee, which added USD $12,250 to the operating income and receivables.

2   For example, it was noted in interviews with Arctic Council representatives that Norway is perceived as paying for the translation of all the Arctic Council's work and websites into Russian and is financially involved in working group projects in the Russian Arctic. It has been difficult to confirm if this perception is fact.

3   As of 2014, the PSI has gained more momentum. The pledged contributions are the following in Euros, and many of the pledges have been deposited into the fund: Finland (200,000 pledged and received); Iceland (8,000 pledged/8,299 received); Norway (238,000 pledged/237,730 received); Russian Federation (10 million pledged/5 million received); Sweden (272,000 pledged/271,565 received); United States (3,782,000 pledged/404,149 received); NEFCO (1,350,000 pledged and received); and Saami Parliament (13,000 pledged/12,987 received). Minor discrepancies exist with some payments due to currency conversion rather than lack of payment; and figures have been rounded off. (Arctic Council Open Access Repository [2014], 2.)

4   The Álgu Fund, newly established by five of the six Permanent Participants (excluding the ICC), aims to help with Permanent Participant funding issues, but it is still new and it is unclear how it has made concrete contributions to help with organizational funding issues at the time of the writing of this book.

3

Institutional Memory and Knowledge Depreciation

Among the many challenges that the Arctic Council has faced, particularly during its first decade, institutional memory and knowledge depreciation have been paramount. Institutional memory issues affect all the Arctic states and inhibit the capacity of the Arctic Council to grow and evolve. In recent years, much effort has been dedicated to tackling this internal challenge. This chapter examines the council's efforts to address institutional memory and knowledge depreciation and looks at the constraints impeding progress toward their remediation. To do so, I focus on delegation formation, specifically the education and term length of representative tenure, and the implications of national variation in delegation formation and term length on regional capacity, efficiency, and unity.

INSTITUTIONAL MEMORY AND KNOWLEDGE DEPRECIATION IN THE LITERATURE

Heidi Hardt, in her article on NATO's institutional memory challenges, defines institutional memory as "shared knowledge within an [international organization] about the outcomes of past crisis management operations" (Haas 1990, 74; Lebow 2006, 3, as interpreted by Hardt 2017, 123). The loss of institutional memory, she says, can have significant implications on an international organization's ability to operate. John Coffey and Robert Hoffman are more precise: "Institutional memory loss is a significant problem that can impact an organization's ability to advance its mission successfully, its ability to avoid making the same mistakes it made in the past, and its ability to leverage the accomplishments of departing employees" (Coffey and Hoffman 2003, 38). Running parallel to institutional memory loss is the occurrence of knowledge depreciation, which Ilhyung Kim and Hae Lim Seo define as "the reverse of learning – unlearning." This, they suggest, "is a phenomenon that occurs when the amount of knowledge gained from experience does not persist but depreciates over time" (Kim and Seo 2009, 1859–60).

Institutional memory loss and knowledge depreciation are major problems for all international forums and institutions. They are among the many factors – the historical context of the relationships between members, national and international agendas, access to resources, pressures to conform to other interests, and pre-existing legal obligations – that explain why actors in forums such as NATO and Arctic Council (Hardt 2017) may approach the same subject differently. While the Arctic states and Permanent Participants may be united in their desire to work on the broad agenda of the Arctic Council, for instance, each of these actors conceptualizes these subjects slightly differently. Richard LeBow explains: "Groups with competing agendas often struggle to shape and control memory on at least the institutional level" (2008, 26).

While organizations face internal competition to shape institutional knowledge and memory, the loss of knowledge, says Linda Argote, has repercussions for the performance of an organization (2013, 58). The most significant consequence of loss of knowledge, she argues, is that organizations will be less productive in the future than they anticipate:

Failure to achieve expected levels of productivity can lead to large problems for organizations … Inaccurate forecasts of future productivity make it very difficult for organizations to plan and organize their internal operations. Further, strategic analyses based on inaccurate forecasts of future productivity can be very misleading. In extreme cases, an organization's actual productivity is so far below its expected or forecasted productivity that the organization is not competitive. (Argote 2013, 58)

If an organization cannot accurately forecast its future aims and output, trust in its ability to follow through on its commitments is undermined. With such trust undermined, the organization will suffer from a loss of legitimacy.

According to Argote broadly speaking, there are two types of knowledge within an institution – structuring knowledge and operating knowledge: "Structuring knowledge describes how to structure or organize operations most effectively, while operating knowledge describes how to perform most effectively within an established structure" (2013, 86). Operating knowledge is often held by workers within an organization who adapt to the environment in which they operate and develop processes that over time become more effective. Structural knowledge, on the other hand, is more embedded in the foundations of a forum or institution and can be found in within an organization's management.

To limit knowledge depreciation, both the structuring and the operating knowledge of an organization need to be protected. If a forum or institution lacks the management structures to preserve knowledge and feed it back into its formal and informal working mechanisms, knowledge transfer at the macro-level is impeded. Similarly, the operating knowledge of daily practices and norms held by workers at the micro-level can take time to develop and can be easily lost when workers leave a work environment. Means of preserving the knowledge gained by workers are necessary.

These two types of knowledge feed into what Argote describes as the three primary causes of knowledge depreciation: "products or processes change and thereby render old knowledge obsolete"; "organizational records are lost or become difficult to access"; and "member turnover" (2013, 73). Since my interviews with representatives to the Arctic Council on this subject frequently revealed challenges of record keeping and representative turnover within the organization, these challenges are the focus of this chapter.

ESTABLISHING A PERMANENT SECRETARIAT

All international bodies suffer institutional memory loss and knowledge depreciation, and these are evident, too, at the Arctic Council. One ongoing example for the Arctic Council is the use of the malleable term "sustainable development." Interviewees commented that competing groups within the council assign the term "sustainable development" different interpretations (English 2013). As a result, representatives of the Arctic states and the Permanent Participants can find themselves speaking at cross-purposes on the subject. Friction due to different understandings of the term introduces tension into discussions, which can in turn influence discourse, cooperation, and even status within the Council.

Argote's reflections on knowledge loss related to the difficulty of finding or accessing organizational records or to the frequency of member turnover strike at the heart of why debates such as the debate over the meaning of sustainable development persist within the Arctic Council. Progress in navigating the sustainable development debate is being held back by problems attributable to issues relating to structuring and operating knowledge transfer.

The Arctic states became aware of these issues early on, realizing that their central cause was the absence of a permanent secretariat for the Arctic Council. The individual working groups each had some form of individual secretariat prior to 2013, but communication among working groups was neither consistent nor well-coordinated. This was in part because they lacked a central hub to act as a data bank and support the controlled transfer of collected data among groups. When combined with the lack of consistent structures to consolidate their work and foster communication, internal competition for resources among the working groups aggravated the problem of institutional memory development.

Although it took some time, seventeen years after the founding of the council, the ACS was eventually established in 2013 (Arctic Council 2013c). Many representatives believed that the establishment of the permanent secretariat was an important step forward for the forum and the working groups (e.g., Former representative to the Arctic Council, 2 September 2016; Former representative to the Arctic Council, 12 October 2016; Representative to the Arctic Council, 19 May 2017). At the same time, representatives also acknowledged the vital importance of the individual working group secretariats (WGS) as part of the structural foundation that makes the forum and the permanent secretariat effective. One representative best summarized the role of the working group secretariats:

> You have the secretariats, which have the continuity and have the institutional capacity ... The assessments are not done by the secretariats and they are not done by the working groups; they are done by the scientists and you have established rules of engagement with the scientific communities as to who does what and how you ensure the credibility of those assessments and how you ensure that you do not jeopardize science while you sort of translate the science into something which has political value ... The functioning secretariats of the working groups, that's where the rubber really hits the road because without that it's difficult to actually do things. (Representative to the Arctic Council, 19 May 2017)

While the working group secretariats were effective for their respective groups, they needed help to coordinate the development of institutional memory at the forum level. Until the establishment of the permanent secretariat, which made it more possible to consolidate, retain, and make available the data and other work of the Arctic Council, the forum lacked consistency.

While the value of secretariats may seem obvious and the omission of a permanent secretariat for the whole Arctic Council apparatus from its inception may seem to have been a design flaw, the decision not to have one was intentional. When the Arctic Council was initially formed, the United States resisted the development of a forum with independent decision-making authority. As a result, a permanent secretariat was not included in the initial forum design (English 2013, 167).

From 1996 to 2013, the ACS rotated from country to country every two years, along with chairmanship of the forum (Johannsson 2013). Consequently, the state holding the position of chair oversaw the secretariat, and personnel changed frequently. Phil Tinline, a writer for the BBC, explains that with staff turnover all workplaces undergo institutional memory and knowledge depreciation: "Each time someone leaves their job, a chunk of the organization's memory leaves too" (Tinline 2016). With the Arctic Council, this loss has been exacerbated by the frequency of the turnover.

Record-keeping practices also varied from state to state. The resulting lack of continuity, and the knowledge depreciation to which it contributed hindered the Arctic Council's evolution and growth. Unable to take knowledge depreciation into account in predictions by the Arctic states and Permanent Participants about the future productivity of the forum (Argote 2013, 81), the rotating secretariat faltered. Without an entity acting as an information hub, the flow of work was impeded, and productivity was slow. The limitations of a rotating secretariat were recognized, and efforts were made to establish a permanent secretariat.

A secretariat was needed to undertake the responsibility of guarding against knowledge depreciation, and to cultivate – and be – the nexus of institutional memory. A place, an object, or a person was necessary to act as an institutional repository. A central institution serves to improve access to information, increasing the efficiency of research, facilitating report writing, for example. Since its creation, the ACS has helped with institutional memory challenges from a procedural and administrative standpoint by, for example, organizing major meetings such as ministerial meetings and updating the Arctic Council's open-access digital repository.

Between 2007 and 2013, the Norwegian, Danish, and Swedish governments "jointly announced an 'umbrella program' for the Arctic Council that would form the common agenda for the three successive leadership terms" (Nord 2015, 29). During the terms of these Scandinavian states, a major part of their agenda addressed "key internal problems that had hindered the organization from becoming as efficient and effective as it had originally aspired to be" (Nord 2015, 30). The crowning achievement of this combined effort was the establishment and funding of the

Arctic Council Secretariat. The permanent ACS formally began during the Swedish chairmanship in 2013. As one high-ranking delegate elaborated:

> When we established the joint secretariat ... the Arctic was still not of any interest to the world in general and when that happened, when the Arctic suddenly [became] the new platform, so to speak, everybody turned their eyes to a small regional organization dealing in environmental issues and sustainable development, and general warm fuzzy feelings, and looked upon it as if it was an Arctic United Nations or something. So if that secretariat had not been in place, the Arctic Council would not at all have been able to receive all that attention. (Former representative to the Arctic Council, 12 October 2016)

The initiative had an undeniable Norwegian imprint, however, and the Arctic states ultimately decided that Norway should host the secretariat. My interviewees suggested that the major factors that contributed to securing Norway the host position for the ACS were Norway's brokerage position with, and geographical proximity to Russia, as well as its history of large financial contributions (see chapter 2) to the forum's work. Norway also committed to be the primary funder of the secretariat.

The key alternative contender to Norway as host to the permanent secretariat was Iceland. In 2013, the same year that the ACS was established (Brady 2017, 178), Iceland subsequently established the Arctic Circle.

> The Arctic Circle is the largest network of international dialogue and cooperation on the future of the Arctic. It is an open democratic platform with participation from governments, organizations, corporations, universities, think tanks, environmental associations, indigenous communities, concerned citizens, and others interested in the development of the Arctic and its consequences for the future of the globe. It is a nonprofit and nonpartisan organization. (Arctic Circle n.d.)

The Arctic Circle has a different focus from the Arctic Council; it acts more as a venue for economic dialogue. However, the initiative sends a strong message about Iceland and its intention to carve out a central place for itself in Arctic dialogue, even though it was not chosen to host the ACS.

The "platform," as the circle is referred to, illustrates Iceland's determination to put itself at the heart of international Arctic discussions. The platform is self-described as having "open democratic" credentials; states, NGOs, and IGOs are all admitted on an equal footing. This statement of democratic-ness and its timing could be interpreted as an initial statement designed to emphasize by contrast the circle's differences from the structure of the Arctic Council. Overall, in the years since Norway was selected to host the ACS, Iceland has been seeking out other avenues to increase its voice in Arctic discussions, using the growing international interest in having input and access to the region to bolster support for its Arctic Circle platform.

EDUCATING REPRESENTATIVES
AND FOSTERING NETWORKS

With the ACS up and running, delegates I interviewed generally observed that the problem of data storage and sharing noticeably improved, drawing attention to the coordinating role of the ACS in daily council practices. Through the establishment of the ACS, the forum had taken important strides toward addressing institutional memory. But another problem became evident: the diffuse nature of state and Indigenous participation in the Arctic Council means that states vary in their methods of educating, selecting, and managing representatives. The knowledge held by individual representatives and the relationships developed between them differ significantly from state to state, in part because of the states' different techniques for representative selection and their personal working relationships with other representatives (Representative to the Arctic Council, 15 September 2016; Representative to the Arctic Council, 14 October 2016; Representative to the Arctic Council, 8 September 2017; Permanent Participant representative,

24 May 2016; Representative to the Arctic Council, 21 June 2016; Former representative to the Arctic Council, 10 May 2016).

Vincent Pouliot observes that, to be of significance, "diplomats must master the local ways of doing things ... If competent practice helps one climb the echelon of multilateral pecking orders, then incompetence should produce the opposite effect" (Pouliot 2016b, 61). Correspondingly, "from a practice perspective ... a country's experience has strong connections with its standing ... it is in and through exposure and repetition that one learns the tricks of the trade" (Pouliot 2016b, 245). If representative postings are too short for them to substantially learn about the Arctic Council's diplomatic dynamics and working practices before moving on to their next posting outside the forum, their states' interests and objectives could be at a disadvantage. Representatives with short postings will not have the time to cultivate the knowledge and the networks necessary for learning and mastering diplomatic practices and effectively navigating the diplomatic environment.

In my interviews, representatives repeatedly acknowledged the value of interpersonal connections and working relationships in fostering the efficiency and effectiveness of the forum's daily work. As one individual commented: "Knowing each other in the working groups personally helps a lot when it comes to the diplomatic work. A lot of issues are handled outside of the meetings, where we discuss something over a cup of coffee ... because we know each other, what organizations we come from, and how to talk to each other" (Representative to the Arctic Council, 21 February 2017). The informal networking aspect of working relationships is also vital at the SAO level, as another representative acknowledged:

The cooperation between the SAOs is very good. Besides the meetings, [a lot of] communication occurs over the internet via emails using very informal language ... It is not very typical for a diplomatic bureaucracy. So, I think it is important. But of course at the end of the day, there are disputes and disagreements between the countries, and you must represent your interests, the views of your political leadership, and even if you think you agree with your colleagues, and they are very agreeable, you must say no. And everyone would understand that, because [it is] a position [that all representatives] have been in at one point or another. (Representative to the Arctic Council, 21 June 2016)

Informal interactions have been acknowledged in practice theory as being usual for diplomatic exchanges among representatives: "informal gatherings allow for the diffusion of various pieces of information, indirectly gleaned through casual conversations with colleagues" (Pouliot 2016b, 128).

One of the major questions facing representatives posted to international forums like the Arctic Council is how to transfer networks and organizational knowledge from one generation of representatives to the next. Long-standing representatives have invaluable insights and experiences that contribute to a forum's success. Unless such information is relayed to an individual's replacement at the end of their tenure, the strength of the bonds among the states within regional diplomacy will be affected.

A major problem with passing institutional memory from one generation of representatives to the next in the Arctic Council is that the forum is not responsible for the selection of state or Permanent Participant representatives. The only group over which the Arctic Council has any say is the staff of its own secretariat. The work and status of the forum, however, is directly influenced by states' delegation selection practices. It is the responsibility of all the actors to select their own representatives; the relatively new ACS cannot – and should not – be tasked with finding, or be expected to facilitate, solutions to this dimension of institutional memory and knowledge depreciation. It is up to the nation-states to work on the education of their own delegations and the transition between representatives.

Theoretically, there would be a correlation between a state's willingness to invest in delegations and that state's standing in diplomatic circles, and the one would ultimately support the other. As Pouliot reflects: "On the one hand, those countries whose diplomatic apparatus is larger would seem to fare better in the hierarchy of standing. On the other hand, governments that rank higher in the pecking order also seem more inclined to invest in their mission" (Pouliot 2016b, 246). The Arctic states would benefit by investing more formally in cultivating the competencies of their delegations. Though some turnover of personnel and resulting loss of memory is inevitable, some states seem less committed, or less able, to invest in maintaining personnel. The issue of maintaining personnel clearly stems in part from organizational or political attitudes toward career progression at the nation-state level.

Besides the potential for impact on a state's standing in various hierarchies, repeated turn-over of personnel is a daily frustration in diplomacy. New representatives consume valuable meeting time on questions that have already been discussed and work that has been completed prior to their involvement. Anecdotally, representatives acknowledged that turnover is less of an issue for the Permanent Participants. The Permanent Participants are seen by their peers as having some of the most knowledgeable representatives in the working groups.

There is a need for the member states to establish entities at the national level to act as historical advisers for their representatives, including SAOs and chairs, in matters of strategy and politics, if relevant institutional memory records or liaisons do not already exist. Such entities or personnel should maintain lists of past representatives from their own state/Permanent Participant organization and other states, as well as information on the representatives' posts, their responsibilities, and the major projects they worked on while part of delegations to the Arctic Council. This information can be gleaned partially from the Arctic Council Open Access Repository, using meeting attendance lists, for example, but no readily accessible list of this information appears to be available (Arctic Council Open Repository n.d.).

For this book, I tried to compile a list of the Arctic Council Working Group chairs (see Appendix 2). This attempt was partially successful. I compiled a draft copy of the chairs using documents from the Arctic Council Open Access Repository, but when I contacted the ACS for assistance in verifying the list, it was revealed that the ACS did not (during the late 2016–early 2018 timeframe of correspondence) have a master copy of this information. I was instructed to contact the secretariats of individual work-

ing groups to obtain verification of the information from each
one. The six working group secretariats also did not have these lists
available, although many individuals from them graciously took
the time to verify my lists after some internal discussion, but some
did not follow up on my repeated requests (a final copy of my lists
of WGS chairs was requested and sent to the ACS upon competition
of this research in 2018). Given how difficult it was to confirm the
identity of people leading the six working group secretariats, it
is likely that verifying the identities of all individuals, the time
periods they spent with the working groups, and the countries
represented by past members of the working groups would be a
major undertaking.

Information retention could be obtained by states and Permanent Participants in additional ways. If entities conducted detailed
exit interviews with their personnel when individuals changed
positions or planned to exit their work for the state or organization, for example, it would help keep track of experts and expertise
as people moved on to other careers or postings after their time at
the Arctic Council. It would also help provide information for
those undertaking the responsibilities of a vacated role going forward if peer shadowing or mentoring was not possible.

The Arctic states need to provide the means (i.e., the funding)
for the Permanent Participants to establish similar institutional
memory-building entities in addition to the IPS. As one Permanent
Participant representative stated:

> The Indigenous Peoples' Secretariat was created by the Arctic
> Council, but it's under the political control of the six Perma-
> nent Participants and, although it was created by the Arctic
> Council and is under the Arctic Council, it is not funded like
> other organizations are. Some countries throw money into it
> and some don't. We have tried for years to create a situation
> where each country would make a contribution, for the core
> funding like the office stuff and to maintain an office. (Perma-
> nent Participant representative, 25 May 2016)

Presently the IPS has a wide range of goals, including:

- To help Indigenous organizations with their Arctic Council work (e.g., "assist and provide Secretariat support functions);
- To enhance capacity of permanent participants (e.g., help "develop their internal capacity");
- To "facilitate dialogue and communication among the permanent participations and among the permanent participants and other Arctic Council and related bodies" (e.g., translation services);
- To support actions "to maintain and promote the sustainable development of Indigenous Peoples culture in the Arctic";
- To gather and disseminate information;
- To raise public awareness of the Arctic Council and its issues (Arctic Council Indigenous Peoples' Secretariat n.d.)

As with the Arctic states and the ACS, representative selection for the Permanent Participants is the responsibility of the individual organizations, not of the IPS. As such, resources are also needed at the level of individual organizations, too, in order to develop mechanisms for institutional memory development.

According to Nord, delegations are most often individuals who go to the Arctic Council and have a lot of experience with Arctic affairs and diplomacy. Sometimes, however, people assigned to the Arctic Council know little about the region before their accreditation. Nord elaborates that group progress can be impeded either by "frequent changes in the personnel attending or by the lack of experience or influence that such individuals may exercise within their own governments or communities" (Nord 2016, 51). This lack of experience was frequently captured in the comments of interviewees. Some council delegates are career diplomats, for example, appointed because of their diplomatic or specialized skills, or as part of a standard diplomatic rotation in their ministry or foreign service, rather than for any region-specific expertise.

A related observation is that the Arctic Council portfolio is in some instances perceived as a stepping stone for a grander posting rather than a career focus area in itself. This perception can also have an adverse effect on the standing of a representative and their state in pecking orders. One consultant to the Arctic Council reflected, for instance, that, in their view, Iceland's presence at the Arctic Council has been affected by the frequency of turnover at the SAO level. The problem, this individual noted, is that there seems to be an inconsistency between Iceland's claim that the Arctic is of primary importance to that country and the general perception that a posting as a SAO is a transition position to a preferred diplomatic posting abroad.

The individuals stated that:

> Iceland has a government that claims that the Arctic is the most important thing for Iceland and they should be very active in participation in the Arctic ... At the same time, the SAOs, they have all looked at being a SAO as a jump to being an ambassador somewhere. So, Iceland in the past ten years has had [something like] 10 SAOs [*a guessed number*]. And if you understand the Arctic Council and that the decisions are made in the coffee breaks and around the lunch breaks, etc. [you understand that] the strength of the Arctic Council is that you can actually talk with the people, and you have the big delegations from the big countries, and then you have the observers there floating around and the Indigenous groups, etc. So, you have access to a lot of people in a very friendly atmosphere, but then at the same time, if you rotate the people too fast, then it's a problem. (Consultant representative to Arctic Council, 14 June 2016)

Although the frequency of changeover among Iceland's top representatives is perceived as problematic, that opinion does not reflect the individual character of those who have held the position. However, it is a perception that these individuals may have to surmount in the eyes of some of their peers.

A continuous rotation of representatives is detrimental to the development of close relationships with counterparts. This can affect representatives' involvement in backroom discussions and the extent to which they are "in the loop" when informal discussions reach the formal negotiating table. On the other hand, Iceland was positively perceived for acting as neutral territory for discussions on Indigenous issues, being the only Arctic state to not have Indigenous peoples. While Iceland is an example of a state that may have turnover issues in the eyes of a few representatives, it is nevertheless well received by others as a proactive and instrumental player in cultivating positive relations between the Arctic states and the Permanent Participants (e.g., Trans Arctic Agenda 2014, 8; Representative to the Arctic Council, 21 June 2016; Representative to the Arctic Council, 21 February 2017).

Representative turnover can also be an issue at the lower levels of the forum. One representative's quick reflection about their first year at the forum gives a sense of the impact of inserting a new person to a job without prior knowledge transfer such as mentorship or job shadowing from the post's previous occupant. As the representative reflected: "I remember my first year or year and a half at the meetings, and I probably obstructed some of the projects [in my working group] because I'd been asking questions that had been discussed a couple of years prior to me being there, so we could have saved the time if I was aware of what had been going on" (Representative to the Arctic Council, 21 February 2017). When I asked what kind of preparation they were given prior to their assignment to the Arctic Council, the representative said "none" (Representative to the Arctic Council, 21 February 2017). Other interviewees, from various levels of the Arctic Council and from different countries, had the similar answer; they had received no pre-assignment education or preparation about the workplace they were entering.

While many delegates noted that they did have access to experienced staff and documents, all of which were valuable as they became oriented as new team members, the value of these resources was at times limited. For example, as several representatives observed, although a new person may have access to experts who can answer their questions, the answers of these experts will only be as good, and as comprehensive, as the question that a new person is able to formulate and ask. Experts may neglect to relay information vital to a representative's work because the representative did not think to ask the right questions.

Tutelage from an experienced mentor can help ensure knowledge transfer and suitability of delegates for the post to which they are assigned. In some cases, representatives had received a great deal of assistance at home and were groomed for their positions (Representative to the Arctic Council, 14 October 2016). Despite the benefits of such an approach, however, few individuals interviewed indicated that this had been their experience (e.g., Representative to the Arctic Council, 21 February 2017; Representative to the Arctic Council, 14 September 2016). Internally, on the other hand, the working groups make a concerted effort to tutor their own leadership and to make sure to share leadership opportunities between delegations and individuals, so that each Arctic state has the chance to chair a working group or a task force at some point (see Appendix of working group chairs for examples).

The selection of working group chairs and vice-chairs to guide the work of the working groups is normally done from within the group. The working group chairs and vice-chairs typically rotate every two to three years, depending on the circumstances. The general idea is that, prior to taking up the position of chair, an individual will first serve as a representative and gain experience with the working group. The chair often has time in a tutelage position of vice-chair, assisting the current chair (e.g., Former representative to the Arctic Council, 12 October 2016; Representative to the Arctic Council, 21 February 2017). This informal tutelage serves to prepare the potential future chairperson, should they assume the position of chair in the future. It also helps to ensure internal working group knowledge transfer, a rotation of country leadership, and continuity in the transferring of chairpersons.

At the SAO level, one high-ranking official reflected that their own preparation for their position was the product of a coordinated effort of tutelage and networking with their predecessor, over a period of years, to ensure their capacity to effectively represent their country's and the Arctic Council's interests (Representative to the Arctic Council, 14 October 2016). Prior to their Arctic Council involvement, this individual spent years in diplomatic service, gaining a strong background in diplomatic work and a broad network base beyond the Arctic region. They then had time to learn about the Arctic Council when assigned to their state's delegation, assisted through tutelage from the person they were set to replace, as was the standard practice in their state. This official felt this method of preparing people in delegation leadership roles provided them with the network introductions and work opportunities to ease into their new position and made them more effective as a representative of their state and of the forum.

In addition to the frequency of turnover, the duration of postings is an important factor that can be linked to the development of institutional memory and efforts to combat knowledge depreciation in organizations. In the Arctic Council there are major differences in the length of time representatives spend as part of delegations and a lot of this variation is linked to which department a representative is from in their home state. This presents challenges to the interactions among delegations and to the forum's capability to operate more broadly. As Linda Argote notes, "turnover not only deprives the organization of the knowledge and skills of the departing member; turnover also disrupts the performance of members who were interdependent with the departing member and had developed relationship-specific assets" (2013, 73).

Reflecting on the issue of turnover, one representative stated:

I think it is very (very) good for us [in the working groups] that there is a continuous experience, and I know for sure that the other delegations, they tend to like that they are meeting the same people more than two meetings, because there is a lot of history, and when you are aware of the history of [a working group] – how it works, who does what and who says what, and thinks what – it makes the work much smoother. (Representative to the Arctic Council, 21 February 2017)

While interviewees also noted that the introduction of new representatives is not a bad thing, as they bring new ideas, it was apparent that the range of preparation opportunities available to help transfer knowledge from experienced representatives to newer members varied considerably. This variation is reflected, for example, in the fact that every country has different ways of assigning individuals to their delegation.

Some representatives from states like the Kingdom of Denmark, Sweden, and Norway, for example, who are assigned from foreign ministries to the Arctic Council, often have about two or three years in their post before moving on or rotating to a new post. This is the usual term length for such postings in these countries and their foreign ministries; it is considered important for career advancement within the different levels of foreign services that individuals not risk stagnation by staying in one posting for too long. This is not an uncommon practice for some states, but short term limits are not universal. Some individuals whom I interviewed had more than ten years of experience working on Arctic issues for their state, but they were not based in the foreign ministries.

The rationale behind short terms is that they give individuals exposure to a wide range of subjects and issues and allow them to contribute new energy and new perspectives. On the other hand, the consequence is that career diplomats subject to these term lengths become generalists – they never become experts in a portfolio or develop deep ties with their counterparts in an organization. Some representatives from the foreign ministries of some of the other Arctic states, however, have many years of experience on Arctic matters and as a result are more likely to have deeper regional networks and experience within the forum to draw upon.

In contrast to the posting process used by Danish and Norwegian foreign ministries, some delegations from the foreign services of Canada and the United States have had representatives with more than three years of experience working on various aspects of Arctic cooperation; some individuals have had five to ten years of experience, or even more. Additionally, Canada and the United States, like the other Arctic Council countries, has delegations made up of members from a range of different federal government departments, such as departments of Natural Resources, Fisheries, Indigenous Affairs, Health, and the Environment. As a result, while some states may have delegates from their foreign services with more restricted time frames on the Arctic Council portfolio, there is a strong likelihood that people from other departments working on other projects related to the Arctic Council have more years of experience.

In comparison to some colleagues from the foreign service, representatives with years of experience working on Arctic issues may lack a current general diplomatic profile. What they can offer instead is a more in-depth familiarity with regional networks, an expertise, and an experiential knowledge of how to navigate the diplomatic norms and structures associated with regional politics. Individuals whose terms working on an Arctic or Arctic Council–specific portfolio are of greater duration may have a more focused worldview compared to career diplomats with multiple postings on their resume, but these experts have valuable region knowledge that could enhance their ability to engage on region-specific topics at a high level, and possibly enable them to use their institutional knowledge as a tool to outmanoeuvre other representatives to advance their agendas. If representatives' terms are short and frequently subject to turnover, however, the depth of the networks these individuals can develop may be adversely affected, given their colleagues' awareness that those with short terms will soon be replaced.

The Arctic states all have different means of selecting their representatives. Some representatives apply and compete for their posting and others are appointed, but there is no consistent approach across all the Arctic state delegations. It is equally important to acknowledge that these methods will have consequences on the greater organization's performance and on the pecking orders of states and representatives within the Arctic Council's diplomatic environment.

CONCLUSION

Overall, the Arctic Council's efforts to deal with its institutional memory and knowledge depreciation issues have led to the establishment of the ACS and the integration of this body into the daily operations of council. The ACS has proven to be a valuable tool for regional cooperation and is instrumental in helping the Arctic states manage the swelling interest in the Arctic Council and international politics in the region (discussed further in chapter 7). It is important to acknowledge, however, that some of the institutional memory and knowledge depreciation issues faced by the Arctic Council result from the way the Arctic states and the Permanent Participants assemble their delegations and prepare their representatives. Consequently, there are significant limitations on how far cooperation within the forum can be used to deal with institutional memory and knowledge depreciation–related challenges. Arctic Council members have different approaches toward preparing their representatives, and national politics, bureaucratic hierarchies, and day-by-day procedures all play a role in fostering these differences.

4

Keeping National Politics
Out of the Forum

It was the window of opportunity offered by the end of the Cold War that made pan-Arctic cooperation possible. During this optimistic period, the Arctic Council emerged, and the Arctic states – and their representatives – made an exceptional effort to include a foundational principle that would allow the forum to be independent of politics beyond the region. In this chapter, I return to the concept of the Arctic Council as a club and illustrate that club status and functioning can be negatively affected when a central foundational principle is contravened.

Deviating from club norms and unwritten rules, particularly those that are perceived to be central to the success of the diplomatic environment, is a major gamble that can destabilize a club's unity, weakening the bond that keeps the voluntary members working together. At the same time, taking such a risk can also affect a state's position within the informal hierarchy of a club. This is not to say that political gambles cannot pay off in diplomacy, but for them to do so, states and representatives must find an adequate balance between club solidarity and national objectives. As Donna Marie Oglesby notes in her book chapter "Diplomatic Language," "diplomats, as political actors, are deeply embedded in a social context that privileges careful, controlled and cautious behavior" (Oglesby 2016, 243).

The effort to keep national politics out of Arctic Council international diplomacy has been an ongoing challenge since the forum's inception. Its success depends largely on those in positions of responsibility. As in other consensus-based clubs, chairmanship roles within the Arctic Council are essentially guardianship posts that can be highly influential if held by an experienced or skilled diplomat. On the other hand, if colleagues perceive those who hold positions of responsibility to be mismanaging their position for domestic political purposes, the way those roles are handled can be detrimental to the status of the individual, the state they represent, and the forum in international politics.

BALANCING NATIONAL INTEREST
AND SYSTEMS MAINTENANCE

According to Iver B. Neumann in his work on diplomatic relations, "diplomacy is about the formulation and pursuit of national interests, and it is about systems maintenance" (Neumann 2011, 576). It is when the pursuit of national interest conflicts with systems maintenance that problems arise.

The Arctic states take great pains to isolate the work of the Arctic Council from issues beyond its mandate or outside the Arctic region; discussion of military matters, as I have mentioned, is explicitly avoided. This careful approach accords with the diplomatic behaviour that Bertrand Badie notes in his work *Diplomacy of Connivance*. Badie reflects that isolationism provides fluidity and inconsistency to diplomatic relations, which helps actors to facilitate relations with other actors who might otherwise be strongly opposed to one another in other diplomatic contexts. As Badie comments: "The fragmented, a-polar system that started to take hold in 1989 is ... characterized by its exceptional ability to create multiple, fluid relations that appear in a given context only to vanish in another" (Badie 2012, 65). The effort required to maintain this protected diplomatic environment and to preserve the integrity of a club's relationships, however, is based on an overarching practice of restraint.

Vincent Pouliot reflects on the problems that can arise when the expression of national interests overrides the obligation for diplomacy: "There are limits to what is acceptable and what is not in the pursuit of one's objectives. The skillful multilateral diplomat must walk a very fine line between getting its way and playing rough-shod" (Pouliot 2016b, 123–4). Diplomats whose performance is seen as maintaining the balance between the pursuit of national interests and a respect for collective endeavour often earn greater standing among their peer group, whereas representatives whose practices are seen not to support the group sufficiently often pay a substantial price for their lack of restraint (Pouliot 2016b, 124–5).

The reason it is so important for diplomats to master the art of balance is that relationships are central to diplomacy. A failure to maintain balance can have untold consequences for diplomats' ability to do their jobs. Disregard for relationships can in turn erode networks, trust in decision-making, and the ability to deliver in negotiations on behalf of those they represent. Donna Oglesby describes the essential relationship-building skills in diplomatic settings:

> Diplomats, above all else, are focused on the process of forming and maintaining relationships with those who manage international relations … Without those relationships, diplomats would find it more difficult to achieve their political objectives or manage crises that may arise over time. To keep the channels of communication open even in times of hostility, diplomats require a non-abrasive manner of communication that lubricates, rounds-off the sharp edges, and creates the space for saving face and creating possibility. (Oglesby 2016, 243)

It is vital for diplomats to master the forms of effective communication expected and needed for them to operate in their environment. Even though developing and maintaining connections takes time, diplomats must stay connected with their colleagues. Such efforts can be confounded by the fact that diplomats' ability to keep channels of communication open can sometimes be strained by forces beyond their control, such as personnel transfers or changes in diplomatic relations among states.

Positions of responsibility being largely guardianship positions, individuals and states who take on chairmanship roles are meant to help maintain "the pecking order using a variety of practices …

that help 'keep the family together'" (Pouliot 2016b, 4; quotations in original text). This obligation of the chair of the Arctic Council is characteristic also of other internal leadership roles in the council (such as that of the director of the permanent Arctic Council Secretariat) as well as those of other international institutions, such as the role of secretary general of the UN.

According to Douglas Nord, who was involved in the Swedish delegation during its years in the rotating chairmanship from 2011–13, "the most important actor ... is the person who is designated to be the chair of the SAO group. This individual not only heads that body, but also orchestrates the other efforts of the chairmanship group and oversees the day-to-day affairs of the Arctic Council as a whole" (Nord 2016, 42). Nord goes on to reflect that:

> The chair can also perform a number of somewhat less visible but equally important informal roles. Perhaps most significant of these is the chair's ability to steer the conversation of the Arctic Council to ... topics and issues of its highest concern. By setting forth the chairmanship program at the outset of their leadership term, the host country can communicate quite effectively which matters it wishes the Arctic Council to focus upon and which it would prefer to give less attention. (Nord 2016, 43)

The relationship between the chair, the SAOs, and the working groups is key to the quality and content of the club's functioning.

In the context of the Arctic Council, however, those holding chairmanship positions have not always lived up to the demands and expectations of their role. At various times during my fieldwork representatives made critical comments about the quality of the chairmanships over the duration of their posting to the Arctic Council. According to a report written for Greenpeace by Terry Fenge and Bernard Funston, communication on the Arctic Council between the top level – chairs and SAOs – and the working groups has been strained since the surge of interest in the Arctic began in the mid-2000s (2015, 16). Fenge and Funston state that, while "communication among working groups have improved, there have been some indications that communications between SAOs and the Working Groups have weakened." By way of context, they add that, "to some degree this situation has arisen as the geopolitical importance of the Arctic has increased and foreign ministries have asserted more control over the Arctic Council agenda and Council messaging, including matters of scientific cooperation" (2015, 16).

These observations echo the opinions expressed by some of my interviewees in 2016 and 2017. Some individuals expressed their disapproval, for example, of the Scandinavian joint chairmanship's move toward discussions focused on economic matters during SAO meetings, at the expense of time discussing environmental issues and research (Representative to the Arctic Council, 13 October 2016). It was Canada's handling of its 2013–15 chairmanship during the 2014 Ukrainian/Crimea conflict, however, that was freshest on people's minds at the time of the interviews, and the issue most discussed when reflecting on the role of the chair in recent years (e.g., Arctic state politician, 20 September 2016; Representative to the Arctic Council, 15 November 2016; Representative to the Arctic Council, 11 May 2016).

For the Arctic Council, the balancing of national and collective objectives is most at play when states are in leadership positions. In these cases, the leadership style of the state will reveal the extent to which it prioritizes national interests over those of the club. If leadership within the club is mishandled, the imbalance can result in a violation of institutional norms, to the detriment of a state's diplomatic responsibilities to the forum's collective agendas. Leadership style and the way it affects the challenge of navigating national and collective interests was a recurrent theme in my interviews.

This theme took centre stage in discussions about the fallout from the 2014 Ukrainian conflict during the period from 2013 to 2015, when it was Canada's turn among the eight states that assume the rotating chairmanship of the Arctic Council. The chair is the public face of the forum during their tenure and sets the forum's agenda for the duration of their term. During its chairmanship of the Arctic Council, Canada was perceived as dragging national politics into regional cooperation.

The central problem with Canada's chairmanship, from the perspective of various representatives from the other Arctic states and Permanent Participants, was that the Government of Canada at that time prioritized national interests and the interests of the political party in power over the collective interests of the forum. One observation was as follows: "Politicians, particularly Stephen Harper, were staunch opponents of Russia's actions against the Ukraine and deliberately dragged Canada-Russian Arc-tic relations into the fray of Canada's response, as most clearly exhibited by Canada's controversial handling of Russia during its chairmanship of the Arctic Council" (Burke and Rahbek-Clemmensen 2017, 402). At a time when it was supposed to be the club's leader, the Government of Canada stopped acting in the group's interest, thereby putting itself at odds with its fellow club members. In accordance with the national agenda of the government of Stephen Harper, Canada tried to leverage its position as chair at the time of the Ukraine conflict, using its chairmanship as a soapbox to target domestic audiences in Canada for political advantage going into a federal election (Burke and Rahbek-Clemmensen 2017, 402).

THE CANADIAN CHAIRMANSHIP
DURING THE UKRAINE CONFLICT

The Ukraine conflict was one of the more sensitive issues that I raised with interviewees, and it was a subject spoken about with a sense of disappointment, particularly with Canada's management of the situation. Interviewees were reluctant to discuss the issue, and very few were willing to be quoted on the subject. All the same, many were open to discussing this matter without direct attribution. This behaviour by representatives is consistent within a club like the Arctic Council, as "in club-style diplomacy, the idea is to survive as an oligarch by covering the errors of one's fellows" (Badie 2012, 22). This is not to say that representatives personally or professionally approved of the Ukraine conflict, but the Arctic Council's mandate excludes discussion of military issues and the forum's norms make violations of the mandate and the forum's norms taboo.

When Government of Canada began condemning Russia during its tenure as chair, it did not follow the script of the expected club behaviour. This deviation was a risk and it upset the balance of the daily practices governing how the club worked – the ways of behaving toward members that help ensure the club's survival and status in international politics. This is not to say that the Canadian representations were unaware of the missteps of their government or chief representative. Quite the contrary; but they were unable to act explicitly counter to the government's position, although some individuals noted that great effort was taken behind the scenes via the chairmanship, to try and caution the government about its rhetoric and politicking. As a result of the government's stance against Russia and its use of the Arctic Council chairmanship to voice its stance, however, the representations appeared to be restricted in their capacity to do their work within the forum.

In diplomacy, "civility is the diplomatic norm [but] a state may choose to violate the norm and make a point by expressing a vehement and overt state-level display of anger in response to a perceived insult" (Oglesby 2016, 246). Canada was not the only Arctic state to indicate its disapproval of Russia's actions within the context of the Arctic Council. The United States, for instance, made its disapproval known when it declined to participate in a meeting of the Task Force for Action on Black Carbon and Methane in Moscow in 2014 (Representative to the Arctic Council, 10 May 2016). Unlike Canada, which also declined to participate, the United States "did not frame its decision publicly as a political act," allowing its message of disapproval to be more subtly expressed. Instead, the United States conveyed its disapproval for Russia's actions in Crimea externally to the context of the Arctic Council, such as by signing executive orders from the president imposing sanctions (U.S. Department of State n.d.) and by criticizing Russia in the context of partnership with allies – through NATO, for example (e.g., NATO Review 2016; Vasovic and Croft 2014). For its diplomatic gamble, Canada was criticized for jeopardizing cooperation within the Arctic Council, not the United States (Exner-Pirot 2016b, 89).

In my interviews with state representatives and Permanent Participants, many reflections on the Ukraine conflict indicated a feeling that the Canadian government had mishandled the situation, but not necessarily the individuals within Canadian delegation. Interviewees gave the impression that the Canadian delegation had to manage the Government of Canada's harsh policy stance against Russia, and that these civil servants had to delicately navigate the tense atmosphere (e.g., Former representative to the Arctic Council, 11 May 2016; Permanent Participant representative, 5 September 2016). The resulting tension made it difficult for Canadian representatives to effectively engage with their counterparts (Exner-Pirot 2016b), particularly as it detracted from their ability to communication with, or have access to, their Russian colleagues and meetings in Russia.

Due to the tense bilateral relations between Canada and Russia, the work of the forum was undermined, and its ability to project regional cooperation as a united front was affected. The encroachment of problems outside the Arctic weakened the club's bond at the time and made it vulnerable to internal struggles and external pressures.

One Permanent Participant representative involved in the forum during that period reflected that:

Canada and Russia [weren't] really best friends at the time and both of them had instructions to not work together ... so when we had meetings in Russia, the Canadians didn't get visas, so they couldn't come, and vice versa. And some of the other countries did not put as much energy into the council at the time also because it was on a pause ... So you could definitely see effects in results and how far you got and what you could actually do with the meetings, because if one country is not represented there [at the Arctic Council] then you cannot really take any decisions or make progress. (Permanent Participant representative, 5 September 2016)

One of the greatest implications of this standstill was that Canada's leadership of the forum came under fire. Its actions were perceived as jeopardizing the carefully nurtured and politically advantageous image of the Arctic states' unity, effectively cooperating to protect the environment and economic opportunities within a "zone of peace" managed by them as a group through the Arctic Council.

The Canadian government was widely criticized for its management of the situation, as was its representation by Leona Aglukkaq, chair of the Arctic Council at the time. Opinions about Aglukkaq's performance were mixed. Although some praised Canada's selection of an Inuk woman for the role of chair, many took issue with Aglukkaq's leadership style. A big part of this opposition was fuelled by her unwillingness to relent on her unpopular and publicly harsh stance against Russia, which was seen as an inappropriate use of her post. In the dense social environments of diplomacy in international forums and institutions, representatives can experience a lot of pressure to conform to the norms and practices of their diplomatic environment. As Pouliot notes, "when the whole group wants to move in one direction, blockers often have a hard time maintaining their stance" (Pouliot 2016b, 126). Aglukkaq, however, would not relent.

High-density social environments foster "the development of local codes and rules, which competent diplomats know how to use" (Pouliot 2016b, 127). These norms in turn influence how diplomats practise their trade. Generally, "diplomats do not usually display fear, disgust, surprise and sadness because they are too personally revealing. But … culturally appropriate somatic expressions are used to show agreement, displeasure, equanimity and anger because they can be effective and do not sever political bonds" (Oglesby 2016, 246). Aglukkaq was not a traditional diplomat and did not adhere to standard diplomatic conduct. With her public and vocal stance against Russia, she was perceived by some of her contemporaries as violating local codes and rules of the Arctic Council and the chairperson role. She seemed incapable, or unwilling, to recognize the problem of taking such an outspoken position against Russia and the conflict that her actions were caus-

ing, particularly since, as chair, she was tasked to facilitate cooperation with Russia.

It is possible that Aglukkaq genuinely believed that taking a harsh
stance against Russia while acting as chair was a legitimate position,
sanctioned as it was by the Canadian government. A key problem
that confronted her was that of audience; who was the target audience of Aglukkaq's condemnations of Russia? And ultimately, whose
interest was she serving – Canada's or the Arctic Council's?

When Aglukkaq tried to signal a position on behalf of the Arctic states and the forum, her actions were perceived as reflecting
domestic interests at the expense of club unity. As a result, she was
perceived to lack the skill to navigate the situation in part because
of the lack of nuance she exhibited in her interpretation of her
government's position against Russia and the way she chose to
express this while chair. As Pouliot states, "the position that states
take and the roles they wish to play in an organization filter
through the instructions that capitals send to their permanent representatives" (Pouliot 2016b, 205) and in this case, the Prime Minister's Office was perceived as being heavily involved.

During her time as the chair, Aglukkaq pushed Canada's "con-
demnation of the intervention in Ukraine." She did so both publicly and in private audiences. For example, Aglukkaq used the visit
of Sergei Y. Donskoi, Russia's minister of natural resources and the
environment, to Canada for an Arctic Council meeting as an
opportunity to criticize the Russian government (Myers 2015). At
one point, Aglukkaq declared Russia's actions in Crimea as "an illegal occupation." She also blamed Russia's military actions in
Ukraine for Canada's subsequent change in approach to Arctic dialogue. For example, news media in Canada reported that Aglukkaq
argued: "As a result of Russia's illegal occupation of Ukraine and
its continued provocative actions in Crimea and elsewhere, Canada did not attend working-group-level meetings in Moscow this
week" (Quinn 2014).

Aglukkaq's role as chair has received attention in academic literature by those reflecting on Canada's chairmanship and its legacy. Heather Exner-Pirot, a Canada-based academic whose work
focuses on international politics and governance in the Arctic

region, observed that Aglukkaq's tenure as the minister for the Arctic Council was seen by some as a "difficult style of management" (Exner-Pivot 2016b, 84). Exner-Pirot goes on to note that some at the Arctic Council meetings felt that Aglukkaq's mandate was beyond her competency, given that she was a federal minister of health and the environment, and the Arctic chair position is typically "held by the Foreign Minister of the hosting state, and the work of the Arctic Council is conducted via foreign ministries and state departments" (Exner-Pivot 2016b, 86). At the same time, however, mirroring feedback that I received from my interviewees, Exner-Pirot states that "others were pleased to see an Inuk lead the Council, the first time an indigenous person had done so and a strong statement not only of Canada's Arctic values but of those of the Arctic Council as well" (Exner-Pirot 2016b, 86).

Aglukkaq's actions were supported by then prime minister Stephen Harper (Burke and Rahbek-Clemmensen 2017, 402) and well received by some segments of Canada's population such as its outspoken Ukrainian diaspora. Aglukkaq's actions, however, were diametrically opposed to the forum practice of trying to isolate itself from external, non-Arctic events, and were out of sync with the internal dynamics in the Arctic Council (for discussion about position-taking in international organizations, see Pouliot 2016b, 206). Canada's position, through Aglukkaq, brought military issues into the forum's diplomatic environment, despite such issues being explicitly excluded within the forum's mandate (Arctic Council 1996). As a result, some of Aglukkaq's counterparts felt she exhibited very poor leadership judgment (e.g., Representative to the Arctic Council, 15 November 2016; Former representative to the Arctic Council, 11 May 2016).

Political gambles like the one taken by the Government of Canada and Aglukkaq tend to pay off when "the pursuit of the national interest must be cast in terms that make sense to the audience" (Pouliot 2016b, 127). However, the audience of Aglukkaq's vitriol against Russia was a domestic, rather than a regional or international one. Many of her contemporaries felt she had threatened and even upset regional cooperation rather than safeguarding it, and despite feedback from colleagues behind closed doors to that effect, Aglukkaq continued to push her stance against Russia while acting as chair. In so doing, she risked damaging the status of the club internationally, as well as lowering her own status and that of Canada within the forum's pecking order.

One representative of an Arctic state summed up the way Canada's strident position toward Russia missed the mark during the Canadian chairmanship.

> We have a unique situation in the Arctic. As much as I can criticize the lack of internal inclusiveness, externally looking at the Arctic Council, it is a good example of collaboration. And the Arctic, regardless of the Arctic Council, is a region that is able to talk to each other, being eight very different states, a number of self-governing nations and many many different peoples, even though there are only four million living in the Arctic. So many cultures living in the same area and no armed conflict, for example. So I'd say, the Arctic is, externally looking from the outside, a very good example of how you can deal with things internationally and not escalate conflict. So that is something you need to be very, very good at taking care of and in that regard, I felt that it was unfortunate that Canada chose at that time to do things differently. (Arctic state politician, 20 September 2016)

The Government of Canada's harsh stance on the Ukraine conflict cast a shadow on Aglukkaq's performance as chair. Among the responses of my interviewees, there was an overwhelming sense that Aglukkaq's capacity to do her job and the positive work of the Canadian delegation were stymied by Canada's insistence on using its chairmanship as a domestic political tool during the lead-up to a federal election, rather than as an opportunity to distinguish itself on the international stage.

Some individuals expressed compassion for the difficulty that Aglukkaq faced in her position, given the level of government interference that she must have experienced. Support for the hypothesis that the Canadian government made Aglukkaq's chairmanship difficult is evident in news reports from that time period. CBC News reported, for example, that in March 2014, the spokesperson for Aglukkaq, Amanda Gordon, stated that Prime Minister Harper had instructed Canadian officials "to review all bilateral interactions with Russia" despite his assurances at the time that "for the moment … Arctic Council work does continue as planned" (CBC News 2014). The government's position later hardened to extent that Canada broke off diplomatic communication with Russia (Westdal 2016), and Aglukkaq had no choice but to operate as chair within the context of her government's actions against Russia.

One former representative to the Arctic Council acknowledged that, in Aglukkaq's position, her manoeuvrability was likely quite constrained by the government.

> If you are an Arctic ambassador then perhaps you don't have anything to do with Crimea so you can sort of go on, but on the other hand you have colleagues who do [deal with Crimea] and instructions on what you can and cannot do, so from my point of view it must have been very difficult for the Canadian chairmanship to handle that. (Former representative to the Arctic Council, 2 September 2016)

In the circumstances, criticism about how Canada handled the chairmanship was directed at the Government of Canada, particularly toward Harper, and the interference by top members of his government.

Criticism directed at the Government of Canada for its approach to regional cooperation was not a new thing. Even as far back as the negotiations to create the Arctic Council in the late 1980s and early 1990s, the other Arctic states and their representatives accused Canada of inserting its own political agenda into council affairs. The "Americans and Scandinavians believed that domestic pressures were pushing the Canadians forward," pressures such as the government's need for a political success after the failure of the Meech Lake Accord and its proposals for constitutional reform (English 2013, 170). In the end Canada's initial proposal for the Arctic Council framework in the early 1990s was heavily criticized and amended by the United States.

Fast forward about twenty years to 2014–15, and there was a similar situation in Canada; an increasingly unpopular Conservative government that had been in power for nearly a decade was caught up in numerous scandals widely reported by the Canadian media (Campion-Smith and Boutilier 2015) and was approaching a general federal election (e.g., Berthiaume 2014; Schwartz 2015). In Canadian politics, nothing is quite as unifying or distracting as Arctic nationalism when it is sparked by credible suggestions that there are threats to Canadian Arctic sovereignty (Burke 2018). The Harper government knew this and had made Arctic protection a central theme during its tenure. Protecting Canadian Arctic sovereignty plays really well in the Canadian media; all you need is an "other," and Russia became the convenient "other" in 2014. Russia's assertiveness in the Arctic, combined with imagery from its Soviet history, and its actions against Ukraine made it perfect for the Harper government to rally Canadians.

The representatives of the other Arctic states were aware of the domestic political situation in Canada and the influence it was having on the Canadian delegation. And they perceived the interference of the Government of Canada, particularly the Prime Minister's Office, in the management of the Canadian chairmanship as a problem. Some felt that if the Canadian government had appointed a more seasoned diplomat as chair, that chairperson might have been able to navigate the situation more effectively (e.g., Representative to the Arctic Council, 14 October 2016). According to some representations, the Canadian chairmanship during this time provides some important lessons for the continuation of the Arctic Council; namely, what the expectations are and the implications of mismanaging the role on an individual's and state's status. One of my interviewees noted that when in the position of chair, it is important for states, and the chair, to remember that they "are brokers," and that taking this stance "is the key to being successful in the chair where you have consensus" (Former Arctic Council chair, 2 September 2016).

If states and their appointed representative undertaking the chairmanship of the Arctic Council lose sight of the need for a del-

icate balance of their dual roles as national and regional representatives while entrusted with the chairmanship, they risk undermining the legitimacy of both the state and the representative acting as the chair. A former chairperson of the Arctic Council
reflected how proceedings can be crippled in such a case:

> When you're trying to put your [national] interests over ours
> [shared regional interests], that's when you know you're really
> close to when things will break down. If that feeling suddenly
> settles, that the chair is disregarding our interests and trying to
> do their own, then you're done as chair. You have no mandate
> to do anything. You can lead meetings, sort of, but your life
> will be very difficult because everything you say will be con-
> trolled and the members have great power over the chair. (For-
> mer Arctic Council chair, 2 September 2016)

A state's standing with its counterparts is constantly in flux and the
good reputation a state and its representatives have cultivated can
be compromised by practices that violate diplomatic norms and
practices. When an actor is seen as violating norms they undermine their legitimacy of in the eyes of those with whom they seek
to cooperate. As a result, states and representatives experience a
negative impact on their position in the internal pecking order of
a club.

CONCLUSION

Those playing a guardianship role for a club, a role such as the
chairmanship of the Arctic Council, are mandated to help safeguard the club. An acquired reputation for unreliability in that
task can have implications for a state's status within the club. This
in turn can affect a state's future capacity to chair and assume leadership in that club. It is important, therefore, that the lessons from
Canada's chairmanship be remembered, particularly by the smaller states in the Arctic Council who do not have the international
standing of the great power actors. The smaller states, and their
representatives, need to be cognizant of the risks of political gam-

bles such as calling for fellow club members to join forces against one of their own. It is important that smaller states stay in tune with the moods of their contemporaries when they propose new ideas. By maintaining a high degree of awareness about the diplomatic environment and the key actors within it, states can minimize the damage they may potentially do to their own status, as well as that of the club, if they take unpopular positions.

5

Language Barriers

Although language barriers are a daily issue for the work of the Arctic Council, there has been a lot of headway in addressing that challenge. This chapter focuses on the features about the club dynamics and pecking orders within it that are demonstrated by the implementation of Russian language services for Arctic Council work. The translation services are available for meeting translators and translations of official documents, and are demonstrated through the availability of the Arctic Council website in Russian, despite English being the working language of the forum. The inclusion of Russian language services is essential for the forum's work, and implementation of these services sends important signals to external audiences about the internal perception of the forum's pecking order, indicating that Russia has an elevated status amongst the Arctic states. Norway has played a major role in making translation services available and has used this position to raise its own status while facilitating the flow of daily operations.

WORKING IN ENGLISH

Even though not all participants in the forum have English as their first language, the working language of the Arctic Council is English. In my interviews with Canadian representatives, I learned that Canada has a policy of translating documents for use within Canada into both French (the other official language of Canada) and Inuktitut. The reasoning behind Canada's domestic process is to increase engagement within various departments and segments of the country, to recognize the language and culture of Inuit peoples in the region, and to help make Inuktitut a working language for Arctic Council exchanges. At the same time, Canada has a reputation of pushing Indigenous issues in the Arctic Council. This stance reflects domestic political interest to better incorporate Indigenous peoples into regional processes, given the inherent legal rights of Indigenous peoples within Canadian politics and law, and the willingness of Indigenous peoples to go to court if they believe these rights are not being respected.

While many languages are spoken by Indigenous peoples and those from the Nordic countries, the main language challenge discussed in my interviews was overwhelmingly the difficulty of engaging with Russian-language speakers. Although engagement with Indigenous peoples in Russia was also mentioned, it was more specifically communication with the delegation from the Russian Federation that was the focus. One of the biggest ambitions of the Arctic states when they created the Arctic Council was to facilitate engagement between the Western Arctic states and Russia. This was made possible after Russia signalled its openness to the process of regional cooperation with Mikhail Gorbachev's Murmansk Speech in 1987 (e.g., Nord 2016; English 2013; Keskitalo 2004), thanks to the relationship-building environment that emerged in post-1989 diplomacy (Badie 2012, 65).

Keeping Russia engaged, however, has been a challenge to the internal dynamics of the Arctic Council. There are many factors that contribute to facilitating open relations with Russia in the Arctic, but as one individual clearly summarized: "Russia's participation is of course very important" (Representative to the Arctic Council, 1 November 2017). Perhaps as a consequence of the need to engage Russia, "Russian translation services are provided, as required, and facilitated by the secretariat of the Arctic Council" (Nord 2016, 43).

Of the eight Arctic countries, Russia is by far the largest, in terms of both geography and population. The need to engage the largest Arctic state is critical to achieving progress toward regional cooperation, particularly since, for much of the twentieth century, the inability to engage with Russia was the central impediment to regional cooperation. Discussions about the possibility of wide Arctic cooperation began just before the end of the Cold War, but it was the implosion of the Soviet Union, the end of the Cold War, and Russia's openness to regional cooperation that opened the door to regional cooperation between Russia and the other Arctic states.

Russia has long been discussed and perceived as the odd one out among the eight Arctic states. As one representative to the Arctic Council observed: "Other than the Russians, the Americans, Canadians and Scandinavians are kind of like-minded. We don't have big fights with Sweden [for example], so yeah, the Russians were always the odd factor [in] how would they react [to regional cooperation]" (Retired Arctic Council chairperson, 7 June 2016). The language barrier feeds into this perception of difference, creating a practical challenge to cooperating with the Russia in comparison to the other states. Unlike the Nordic countries, where many people learn English as a second or third language, the Russian representatives and scientific experts often did not speak proficient English in the early years of regional cooperation. Some still do not have a professional proficiency in the language, although more Russians are now seen to have a conversational proficiency that has opened networking opportunities.

The IPS assists the Arctic Council Secretariat with translation services (Arctic Council Indigenous Peoples' Secretariat, n.d.) and, as chapter 2 illustrated, its budget is funded primarily by Norway and the Kingdom of Denmark. These services include: arranging translator services at key meetings (SAO meetings and ministerial meetings) in working groups (where possible); translation of main Arctic Council documents, such as the "agendas, meeting reports, key reports and report summaries"; translation of outreach materials and the Arctic Council website; and "other Russian language-related support as instructed by the Director [of the ACS]" (Arctic Council Secretariat Preliminary 2015 Annual Report 2016, 20–1).

These services are important within the forum for at least two reasons. First, to support the engagement and participation of Russian representatives. As one senior representative noted:

Language is certainly an issue in some work of the council. While English is the operating language of the council, there are best efforts made to make Russian a second language. Certainly, at all high-level meetings, interpretation is provided. There is a Russian speaker in the Arctic Council Secretariat, there are some delegates from other countries that speak Russian, and while it is not the easiest place for a unilingual Russian to attend, it's not impossible. (Representative to the Arctic Council, 10 May 2016)

Second, providing translation services to the Russian delegation, rather than Russia having to arrange to provide and pay for the service, highlights the keen interest of the other states that they must work with Russia and they must commit to making the professional relationship work. It also highlights Norway's focus on Russia and its anticipation of Russian needs.

Delegates I spoke to for this book generally felt that the English of the Russian delegations had improved over the past twenty years. Individuals who have had longer postings to the Arctic Council added that Russian representatives now appear more at ease conversing in English in informal settings compared to their earlier experiences with them. Even as the ability of Russian representatives to converse in English improves, however, there has been no discussion about discontinuing the translation services. Rather, the act of providing the service has become embedded in the daily practices of the forum's work and remains an essential component in demonstrating interest in maintaining Russian participation.

Giving Russia special attention within the forum is an effective way of fulfilling a key focus of the Arctic Council; namely, open and positive dialogue with Russia. Much of the environmental clean-up and protection work that was done in the early years of the Arctic Council focused on the Russian Arctic because that state was saddled with a legacy of environmental problems as a result of its heavy use of the region during the Soviet era (e.g., Bloom 1999; Arctic Council 2011b). Without open and positive dialogue, such work would not have been possible.

NORWAY AS A BROKER

Formally, "Norway's support of the Russian language in the Arctic Council is motivated to help facilitate their participation" (Representative to the Arctic Council, 1 November 2017). Norway's closeness with Russia, however, was a very common theme in my interviews. People would often take note of the skilled way in which Norway navigated both its diplomatic and its security relationships with the West and with Russia. As one retired diplomat who had been stationed in Russia reflected:

> It is very interesting to look at Norway's relations with Russia. The Norwegians live beside the Russians. They invest in deterrence; they joined NATO, they're buying F-35s, they have an awful lot of money, the Norwegians, for a change in their history. But they take Russia very seriously and they invest a lot of talent in sustaining and understanding Russia. They invest in Russian language studies, Russian history studies; they sustain a cadre of Russian specialists in their foreign service and they try to sustain a dialogue with Russia despite other tensions. (Retired Arctic state diplomat, 9 May 2016)

The fact that Norway volunteers to pay for Russian translation services highlights Norway's brokerage behaviour. The position of broker is valuable, and Norway is notable for repeatedly putting itself in that position. Brokers are powerful actors in diplomacy because they "occupy central positions in networks, meaning that they have stronger connections with more than one cluster" (Pouliot 2016b, 141). Norway's keenness to embed itself as a key broker in the Arctic Council is not a practice isolated to the Arctic region. Norway often uses its wealth and its diplomatic astuteness to integrate itself in the heart of international issues (Lahn and Rowe 2015, 135–6).

Norway's cultivation of a brokerage position is not a signal that Norway is seeking to navigate toward a status position on a par with Russia and the United States. According to Benjamin de Carvalho and Jon Harald Sande Lie, authors of "A Great Power Performance: Norway, Status and the Policy of Involvement," many small states accept the fact "that they are likely never to become a great power." Instead, as de Carvalho and Lie note, small states "compete for status with their peers for good-power status" (De Carvalho and Lie 2015, 69).

Norway's decision to pair its interest in Arctic cooperation with substantial financial commitment has given it one of its key tools to compete regionally, and its contribution extends well beyond offering translation services. As one senior representative noted:

> For Norway, the Arctic Council has been a priority for a long time. That would just be an empty statement if it was not backed up by some support, financial support, and I think it is something Norway has chosen to do, to support the Arctic Council with financial resources. Not only with regard to translations to Russian but also in other areas. So, I think that when the Secretariat became permanent in Tromsø, it was expected that Norway would support that a bit more and that as the host country it would in a way be expected that Norway would support it a bit more than the other members. Also, when the IPS [Indigenous Peoples' Secretariat] moved from Copenhagen to Tromsø, it was expected that as the host country Norway would contribute more (Representative to the Arctic Council, 1 November 2017).

Norway is playing to its strengths by integrating itself as an invaluable component of regional cooperation at a deeper level than other small states; this helps it create niche competencies vis-à-vis Russia.

This behaviour on Norway's part has been evident for decades. It is rooted in Norwegian perceptions of threats to its national security and the way the country situates itself in international politics (Rottem 2007). During the Cold War, for instance, Norway was a key NATO ally in Europe, while at the same time skillfully managing its delicate position bordering Russia and the Warsaw Pact nations (e.g., Græger 2005, 88). Norway withstood pressure from its NATO allies to permanently station troops in its territory, in order to resist antagonizing the Soviet Union (Allport 2017), and adopted a mixed policy toward the Soviet Union, one characterized by deterrence and reassurance. Part of this policy included maintaining a "ban on foreign military bases on Norwegian territory in peacetime" (Rottem 2007, 628).

Norway is not the only Arctic state to act in such a clearly calculating and practical manner to balance its geostrategic placement between two much larger powers. Representatives and diplomats also noted that, among the Arctic states, Finland has behaved in a similar manner. Finland, however, has a smaller economy and lacks Norway's oil resources as a source of revenue. Norway's estimated GDP in 2017 was USD $375.9 billion (*World Factbook* n.d.; see Statistics Norway 2018), whereas Finland's GDP in 2017 was USD $242.4 billion (*World Factbook* n.d.; see Finnish Government 2017). Norway also has its Arctic coastal state status to help further regional interests (discussed further in chapter 8).

Like Norway, Finland shares a land border and history with Russia, which has sharpened its awareness of its neighbour and its need to look out for its own security and strategic interests in a practical and self-reliant way. This hyper-awareness of Russia is part of the reason that Finland was paying so much attention in the 1980s and was quick to seize the opportunity of cooperation with Russia presented in the Murmansk Speech. Finland also acted as a broker to bring together the Arctic states as the genesis of regional dialogue, spearheading the development of the Arctic Environmental Protection Strategy in the late 1980s and early 1990s, which later contributed to the development of the Arctic Council.

Now, with regional cooperation up and running in the post–Cold War era, Norway's brokerage mentality stands out, evidence of it is apparent keenness to host the Arctic Council's Permanent Secretariat (ACS) in Tromsø, in Northern Norway. While acting as the host, the Government of Norway pays for a major share of the ACS and the IPS. The Norwegian foreign ministry also pays for Russian translation services, but as with most Arctic Council funding, it is hard to obtain a clear account of how much these services cost. The only thing that is clear is that Norway is financially backing all translation services, either wholly or in part, depending on where those sources are being accessed.

The Arctic Council's 2015 Preliminary Annual Report states: "The Russian translation service is funded by the Norwegian Ministry of Foreign Affairs" (Arctic Council Secretariat Preliminary 2015 Annual Report 2016, 20), but the ACS provides these services, as does the IPS. The IPS, for example, helps "facilitate the translation of the communication between the Permanent Participants" and ensures that "communications are in both English and Russian" in order "to effectively communicate with the Russian Indigenous Peoples" (Arctic Council Indigenous Peoples' Secretariat n.d.).

What is not clear is whether the funding that Norway has contributed for translation services is supplementary to its funding for the ACS and the IPS. It is also unclear whether the IPS services come out of its budget, to which Norway contributes an estimated 50 per cent, with the Kingdom of Denmark as the other major contributor (Permanent Participant representative, 24 May 2016). Either way, Norway is funding the translation service initiative.

The desire to make this extra effort for Russia also highlights Russia's high status within the Arctic region; Russia receives additional services when other state representatives and Indigenous peoples do not. Norway's decision to fund Russian translation services sends a multitude of messages about both Norway and Russia. Many people I interviewed spoke very highly of Norway and its commitment to making the Arctic Council succeed. Many comments were made about the extra effort that Norway puts into engaging and understanding the Russians. A retired diplomat who spent years in Russia and Eastern Europe, for instance, noted that the Norwegians push themselves to keep relations good with Russia, but they are also invested in deterrence and are very aware that things could turn bad for them really quickly if Russia wanted to be militarily aggressive (e.g., Retired diplomat, 9 May 2016; Retired diplomat, 11 May 2016).

The Norwegians use their relatively newfound wealth as a multifaceted tool to open many doors. Bård Lahn and Elana Wilson Rowe, authors of "How to be a 'Front Runner': Norway and International Climate Politics," note that Norway was the leading contributor to the voluntary United Nations Framework Convention on Climate Change (UNFCCC) fund. This fund is meant to enable the UNFCCC "to organize negotiating sessions and finance developing country participation in meetings" (Lahn and Rowe 2015, 136). Lahn and Rowe note that "Norway has used its 'comparative advantage' as a wealthy nation to take on the role of the generous economic contributor to climate change mitigation efforts in general, the UNFCCC negotiations in particular" (Lahn and Rowe 2015, 135). From 1 January 2008 to 15 November 2012, Norway was the highest contributor to UNFCCC, giving USD $20,587,842. This contribution surpassed those of the Kingdom of Denmark (USD $15,262,630), the United States (UDF $14,334,850), and the EU (USD $13,335,601). Norway's investments, Lahn and Rowe argue, help it "gain recognition as a bridge-builder and facilitator" (Lahn and Rowe 2015, 136).

Norway's wealth is its greatest tool of self-defence, and it is concerned about defending its interests as well as its borders (Retired diplomat, 9 May 2016). Engagement with Russia is part of its overarching protection plan. Diplomats and representatives point out that Norway is extremely important in engaging Russia in the Arctic and express admiration for the skill employed by the Norwegian foreign ministry in working so well with their Russian counterparts.

A diplomat who also spent years posted in Russia from one of the other Arctic states commented:

> The ones I have always admired for being the leaders in dealing with the Russians are the Norwegians. They know what's going on in Russia. They have a far better understanding of what's going on in Russia compared to what we do because they have a lot of Russian speakers in their foreign ministry ... and they have this system because they are a small country, they have been watching Russia for so many years. The young people who join the Norwegian military are trained in Russian and they eventually transfer to the Foreign Ministry and other establishments so you have a very large pool of Russian speakers in Norway and of course they are neighbours and they have

had all this border trade with Russia over the years ... their understanding of Russia is far greater, and they understand the capital importance of Russia in their foreign policy and in terms of their own national interests. (Retired diplomat, 11 May 2016)

Representatives do not see Norway's investment as altruistic. They see it as grounded in two main points – necessity and self-interest. Norwegians "understand Russia" because they have to in order to work with their large neighbour. Similarly, the Norwegians are seen as "good at defending their own interests," in terms of both economy and security (Retired diplomat, 11 May 2016).

Throughout the Arctic, Norway is repeatedly described as "practical," and its bond with Russia is typified as a continuation of this practicality. As one individual observed, "Norway and Russia have interests that bind them together and not in an emotional way" (Representative to the Arctic Council, 15 November 2016). Norway's practical nature, shared by Finland and the other Scandinavian states to a lesser extent, can be observed by its counterparts in Norway's Arctic relations, especially when it comes to working with Russia. One retired diplomat noted that: "The Finns and the Norwegians, and even the Swedes and the Danes to some extent, are very practical [when it comes to Russia] ... Unlike other countries, the Norwegians and the Finns were not afraid of Russia: 'we're neighbours, if we were to be afraid we couldn't live, so we entertain, we discuss' ... They have known how to deal with Russia in a way that we have not" (Retired diplomat, 11 May 2016). The policy of supporting language services can be seen as another avenue through which Norway is acting practically to integrate itself as a broker between Russia and the West; literally facilitating smoother communication.

This provision of translation services also helps Russia by conveying a message about Russia's status within the club; it says something about Russia that it did not need to pay for its own translation services. Successful engagement with Russia is a given for regional cooperation to work and this was stressed on numerous occasions (e.g., Permanent Participant representative, 24 May 2016; Permanent Participant representative, 25 May 2016; Representative to the Arctic Council, 30 May 2016).

To give some sense of how essential Russia's participation is to Arctic cooperation, many representatives strongly believe that without Russia regional cooperation in the Arctic Council would not function. This valuation is truer of Russia than the other Arctic states, with the possible exception of the United States. John English reflected that those dynamics existed even when the forum was being established: "all Arctic states knew that the Russians and the Americans mattered most, each had an implicit veto of the proposed council" (English 2013, 226).

Comments from representatives, both on and off the record, strongly indicate that keeping Russia at the table in the Arctic Council is a necessary part of the forum's success. Comments included:

> What would happen to the Arctic Council if Russia left? It would collapse. It would absolutely collapse. Most of [the Arctic] is Russia, so how could you have an Arctic Council without Russia being there and participating in it? You have to have the eight. (Permanent Participant representative, 24 May 2016)

> I think it's important, even though it does take some finesse and maybe compromising your goals at least in the short term to keep them in, to keep the Russians in. They are the biggest group. How can the Arctic Council work without it, if more than half of the Arctic leaves the organization? I don't think it can. (Permanent Participant representative, 25 May 2016)

With the desire to keep Russia at the table so high, Russia's status in the club, and by extension internationally, is relatively high in both international and regional hierarchies. Providing translation services might be a practical matter in terms of daily operations, but it also sends the very real signal that working with Russia not only requires an extra effort but is worth the extra effort.

CONCLUSION

Overall, addressing the language barrier between the Russian representatives and the rest of the Arctic state representatives has made Arctic cooperation more productive. Norway's facilitation of translation services reflects positively on Norway for its role as facilitator; and it sends a positive signal to Russia that its participation is worth the provision of such a service. For Norway, "brokering is a significant source of standing and influence because it renders others dependent on the broker for their interactions" (Pouliot 2016b, 141). To date, Norway has successfully cultivated its status as a broker in Arctic cooperation. The identification and management of language barriers between the Russian delegation and the others within the Arctic Council is one way in which Norway has acted within the framework of regional cooperation to consolidate the brokerage status it has cultivated.

PART TWO

Introduction to External Challenges

The Arctic states' determination to address daily challenges to the Arctic Council's work extends beyond their efforts to deal with internal challenges. As a club, they face external challenges in addition. These challenges have an effect both on the forum's internal practices and on the capacity of the Arctic states to maintain the forum's status in international politics. In Part Two, I argue that Arctic states are aware of how external challenges to the Arctic Council's daily practices can affect the council's international status. Consequently, over the past decade they have made considerable efforts to address such challenges.

According to a former representative, Russia's planting of a titanium flag under the Polar Ice Cap on the seafloor location of the North Pole in 2007 was instrumental in triggering international awareness of and subsequent interest in the Arctic region (Former representative to the Arctic Council, 12 October 2016). The incident drew attention to possibilities for change and opportunities in the region. In particular, it focused international interest on the broader, more substantial subjects of climate change and the environmental risks and economic possibilities emerging in the Arctic. This increased interest had two principal implications. The first, as Olga Khrushcheva and Marianna Poberezhskaya note in their work on the Arctic in the political discourse of Russia, was that "after the 'flag' incident, Russia turned towards a more cooperative policy by accepting bilateral and multilateral agreements with other Arctic nations" (Khrushcheva and Poberezhskaya 2016, 551). The second was the Danish-led drive for the Ilulissat Declaration, a statement from the five Arctic coastal states which sought to send a clear and concise message that the Arctic region is "not unclaimed territory and is not a Wild West" frontier (Former representative to the Arctic Council, 12 October 2016).

The Ilulissat Declaration was intended to signal to the international community that it had misunderstood the Arctic and failed to recognize the existence of the international jurisdictional framework that covered the region (Bloom 2009, 372–3). The declaration also served to remind the world about the established national territorial sovereignties governing the Arctic region (e.g., Steinberg et al. 2015, 1; English 2013, 1–2).

Some have described the region's internal political dynamics as a "Great Arctic Game" unfolding in the region, with Arctic states plotting to expand in a nineteenth-century-like manner with a scramble for territory and resources with such symbolic gestures as flag-planting (Khrushcheva and Poberezhskaya 2016, 547). Descriptions of that sort illustrate important dimensions of Arctic politics and dynamics of Arctic Council cooperation. Any disagreements over maritime boundaries and the status of certain waters and waterways in the Arctic are largely viewed by the Arctic coastal states as internal regional political matters. Such bilateral disputes – disputes over the legal status of waterways (Northwest Passage and Northern Sea Route) and continental shelf extension claims – are not, however, subjects discussed within the Arctic Council. These disputes all involve the same political players, but mainly occur bilaterally, and the Arctic states have little interest in opening up their own regional boundary disagreements for outside interference.

The external political pressures on the Arctic Council which were most prominently highlighted by representatives during my interviews were: communication with outside audiences; managing the admission and participation of observers; and pressure for the Arctic Council to become an institution based upon a treaty rather than a consensus-based forum. The following chapters examine these challenges by exploring their causes and the way they have affected the club dynamics of the Arctic Council, and ways in which they are being addressed by the council and its member-states.

6

Communication and Misunderstandings

Communicating on a wider scale about the Arctic Council's existence and work has been a more recent challenge for the forum (e.g., Haavisto 2001; Graczyk 2012). In my discussion of language barriers in the previous chapter, the implied definition of language was as a form of spoken and written communication. The content and means of communication within and beyond the Arctic Council – language in a broader sense – also demands our consideration. As Wilfred Dolfsma, author of *Institutions, Communication and Value*, states, "conceptualizing the durability and change of institutions is only possible through acknowledging the role of language" (Dolfsma 2009, 14). When actors initiate communication, they work within accepted rules and norms, but nonetheless, successful communication cannot be not guaranteed. An actor's comprehension of the rules and norms they draw upon "can be incomplete, or incompletely or differently understood, even within a single community" (Dolfsma 2009, 15).

The need for more coherent communication to external audiences about the Arctic Council became especially apparent in the wake of the 2007 Russian flag-planting media stunt, which focused a spotlight on the impact of climate change and the presence of new economic possibilities emerging in the region. Concern about climate change and its impact on the Arctic dates back to the 1980s and 1990s, during the negotiation of the Arctic Environmental Protection Strategy but, with the creation of the Arctic Council, climate change became a priority area for regional dialogue and cooperation (Koivurova and Hasanat 2009, 63–4). An early example of the Arctic Council's focus on climate change is evident in the publication of the 2004 *Arctic Climate Impact Assessment Synthesis Report* (ACIA) (AMAP: Arctic Climate Impact Assessment n.d.).

The ACIA report highlights "prevailing trends of climate change in the region and the implications of Arctic warming for the rest of the world" (Koivurova and Hasanat 2009, 66). It stresses that climate change does not occur in isolation but has widespread implications:

> The impacts of climate change will occur within the context of the societal changes and pressures that arctic indigenous residents are facing in their rapid transition to the modern world. The imposition of climate change from outside the region can also be seen as an ethical issue, in which people in one area suffer the consequences of actions beyond their control and in which beneficial opportunities may accrue to those outside the region rather than those within. (Arctic Climate Impact Assessment 2005, 4)

The ACIA helped to inform the Arctic states on the serious implications of climate change and "by 2005, all Arctic governments and many others had come to officially accept that climate change was melting the Arctic ice cover, which meant that the Arctic was becoming more accessible both to the Arctic states and to the international community" (Huebert et al. 2012, 2).

It was only two years later, in 2007, that Russia used a mini-submarine to plant a titanium Russian flag on the sea bed of the North Pole. The incident received a massive amount of international media attention and fed into a rapidly growing belief at the time that there was a rush to claim the Arctic and its natural resources. The BBC News, for instance, ran a story with the tagline: "Russian explorers have planted their country's flag on the seabed 4,200m (14,000ft) below the North Pole to further Moscow's claims to the Arctic" (BBC News 2007). Reuters' coverage of the flag planting had a similarly provocative opening statement: "Russian explorers dived deep below the North Pole in a submersible on

Thursday and planted their national flag on the seabed to stake a symbolic claim to the energy riches of the Arctic" (Faulconbridge 2007). The *New York Times* continued the theme of the Russian land-grab and resource claims: "The dive was a symbolic move to enhance the government's disputed claim to nearly half of the floor of the Arctic Ocean and potential oil or other resources there" (Chivers 2007).

While the incident is symbolic of Russian Arctic capabilities and its claims to a portion of the Arctic region, which extend up to the North Pole and of which all the Arctic states were aware, the incident sparked international fascination with the Arctic region and its economic potential, though at a very basic level. It quickly became apparent from the news coverage that journalists and readers did not know much about the Arctic region. The flag-planting incident acted as a catalyst for international attention to the Arctic and forced the Arctic states to improve their communication related to the region (see Khrushcheva and Poberezhskaya 2016; Burke and Rahbek-Clemmensen 2017).

One of the main implications of this additional attention was that it made the Arctic states more aware of the need to do something about their communication about the Arctic region. It became apparent that their perceptions of the region – such as the jurisdictions of the Arctic states and the nature of regional cooperation and governance – were not in line with the way those outside the region perceived or conceptualized the Arctic and their ambitions for access to it. The Arctic Council, in particular, is misunderstood and was initially seen by those newly interested in the Arctic region as an institution with a far broader focus and authority than it had. The disconnect between the international understanding of the Arctic Council, and the Arctic states' own perception of the region posed a risk to the regional leadership status of both the forum and Arctic states. This realization motivated the Arctic states to begin to modify their communication practices, both individually and as a group (through the Arctic Council).

As far back as 2001, the Arctic Council was aware that its communication needed to improve if the forum was to survive and prosper. The 2001 Haavisto Report highlighted communication as a core challenge to the forum under the heading, "Nobody knows exactly what is going on in the Arctic Council" (Haavisto 2001, 34). The report elaborated: "The Arctic Council is an international forum, not an international organization, but due to the current structure nobody can provide an answer to what are the activities that are ongoing in the Arctic Council. This is due to the poor communication between the Working Groups, weak contacts from the Working Groups to SAOs, and a lack of institutional memory in the Council" (Haavisto 2001, 35). After the 2007 Russian flag-planting incident, the forum increased its strides to address this challenge, because past communication practices were discovered to have contributed to misunderstandings about the Arctic region and its governance, and what the Arctic Council was doing.

Many of these changes were initiated during the 2011–13 Swedish chairmanship. The Swedish chairmanship was led by Gustaf Lind and is noteworthy for the establishment of the Arctic Council Secretariat (ACS) (with Norway and the Kingdom of Denmark) and for its coordination of information outreach. A good example of outreach was the introduction of the Arctic Council Twitter account. Overall, influences such as increased awareness of the impact of global warming on the Arctic and the resulting increase of interest in the region from outside actors, have kickstarted efforts by the forum to send signals about its work and its purpose both to Arctic state audiences and further afield.

The existence of diverse opinions about the Arctic region has been fuelled by the Arctic Council itself and its failure to actively articulate their vision of the forum. In its first decade, few people and actors outside of the forum knew much about it. The joint involvement of the eight Arctic states, six Permanent Participants, and a handful of observers was an unusual arrangement in international forums for its time. The Arctic Council was notable for the way in which it included Indigenous peoples and cooperated with the emerging Russian state after the dissolution of the Soviet Union. The council's tardiness in its public relations approach has had a significant influence on the kinds of external pressures that the forum faced from non-Arctic states and non-governmental actors in recent years, and in turn has had an impact on its efforts to respond to these pressures.

COUNTERING THE SHOCK
OF THE 2007 FLAG-PLANTING INCIDENT

In its first decade, the Arctic Council was a quiet affair, its existence relatively unknown. In 2007, however, the Arctic Council and region were thrust into the international spotlight. After having had a very limited international profile, the Arctic Council and its key members were taken aback by the sudden interest. The major fallout of the 2007 Russian North Pole flag-planting incident for the Arctic Council and the Arctic states was that they were bombarded with attention by non-Arctic actors and the international media. The incident stimulated pressure both from states and from non-governmental organizations for greater involvement in, and access to the region. The council's permanent members – the Arctic states and Indigenous peoples' organizations – had not anticipated this increase in attention, or pressure, and were not immediately prepared to address it.

The attention received by the Arctic Council from outside actors of all stripes in the mid-2000s was often driven by misconceptions – that the Arctic region lacked a jurisdictional framework, that the Arctic states were challenging each other over resources, and that the region is a global commons. The misconceptions also included misunderstandings about the purpose of the council since it was the only regional forum, and it came to be seen as a United Nations–type arena for the Arctic region. Actors did not initially understand what the Arctic Council was designed to do.

The Arctic coastal states in particular were distressed by misinterpretations about the Arctic Ocean. They were motivated to draft the Ilulissat Declaration in 2008; a declaration made by the five Arctic coastal states – Canada, the United States, Russia, Norway, and the Kingdom of Denmark (Ilulissat Declaration 2008). The Ilulissat Declaration was a successful attempt to dispel what the Arctic coastal states saw as the misapprehension that the Arctic Ocean was a free-for-all space, open for outsiders to stake claims. Rather than being an unclaimed area, only 20 percent of the Arctic region and the Arctic Ocean are considered "international commons in international law" (Fenge and Funston 2015, 7).

While reminding the world that the law of the sea also applied to the Arctic Ocean, the declaration also strongly signalled that there is a pecking order within the Arctic region and the coastal states – Canada, the Kingdom of Denmark, Norway, Russia, and United States – are at the top of this hierarchy. The Ilulissat Declaration declared the following:

By virtue of their sovereignty, sovereign rights and jurisdiction in large areas of the Arctic Ocean the five coastal states are in a unique position to address these possibilities and challenges ... Notably, the law of the sea provides for important rights and obligations concerning the delineation of the outer limits of the continental shelf, the protection of the marine environment, including ice-covered areas, freedom of navigation, marine scientific research, and other uses of the sea. We remain committed to this legal framework and to the orderly settlement of any possible overlapping claims ... This framework provides a solid foundation for responsible management by the five coastal States and other users of this Ocean through national implementation and application of relevant provisions. We therefore see no need to develop a new comprehensive international legal regime to govern the Arctic Ocean. We will keep abreast of the developments in the Arctic Ocean and continue to implement appropriate measures (Arctic Ocean Conference 2008).

The decision to draft the Ilulissat Declaration, though technically not negotiated within the Arctic Council, was important for the Arctic states and their status in regional politics.

The declaration demonstrated unity in a quick and concise manner and it illustrated the willingness and ability of the Arctic states to push back against external pressures seeking to encroach on their region. It also illustrated the hierarchical divisions between coastal and non-coastal states which existed in regional politics, and the difficulty in thinking of ways to incorporate Indigenous peoples' organizations into discussions that traditionally take place between states.

This example of early, but decisive, resistance to outside ambitions for the Arctic did a lot to quell outside momentum. Robert Jervis notes that "if small gains and losses lead to larger ones, it is obviously important to stop the bandwagon before it gathers momentum" (Jervis 2017, 247). The maxim that "early resistance is cheaper and safer" is supported by a number of factors: first, "conquests can add to the aggressor's physical strength"; second, "the adversary's initial probes may be tentative" but if the defender retreats then "expecting similar behavior in the future, [the adversary] will become bolder and can be stopped only by stronger resistance"; and finally, "probes can be turned to the defender's advantage" (Jervis 2017, 248). The Ilulissat Declaration swiftly corrected lingering views that the Arctic states were fighting each other over resources, or that the Arctic region was open for external sovereignty or resource claims; the Arctic is not the Wild West and it is an inhabited space.

In the course of communicating, says Jervis, "most communications convey two messages: what the actor is saying and the fact that he needs to say it" (Jervis 2017, 111). Dual purposes of this sort are very evident in the publication of the Ilulissat Declaration. Steinberg et al. comment that the declaration "was notable in that it broke absolutely no new diplomatic or political ground [but] the point of the declaration [was] to assert that there was a status quo, that it was functioning fine and that there was no need to change it" (Steinberg et al. 2015, 1). The declaration was not a statement of intention or a declaration of new claims; rather, it was a reiteration of fact from the point of view of the Arctic Five states. It is significant that the declaration came from the Arctic Five, and that they were the group that was pointing out that international perceptions of the Arctic were incorrect. The declaration was a means of symbolically presenting a united front. Through the Ilulissat Declaration the Arctic coastal states were also able to undercut any competing message that the region was *terra nullius*. The Arctic Five also conveyed the message that they were the Arctic states in charge of maritime issues, thereby suggesting that their position among the Arctic states was elevated over the non-coastal states in the internal pecking order.

THE @ARCTICCOUNCIL JOINS TWITTER

By the time of the Ilulissat Declaration, the Arctic Council had been in operation for over a decade and had established ways of doing things. According to Andrew F. Cooper and Vincent Pouliot, in their examination of internal diplomatic practices among the G20 countries: "Practices are socially meaningful and organized patterns of activities stemming from a know-how that is generated over time. Practice rests on established ways of doing things ... Practices structure interactions and that is arguably why they tend to exhibit some regularity over time ... Patterned ways of doing things produce mutual expectations, facilitate coordination and render communication possible" (Cooper and Pouliot 2015, 336). Despite its established practices, however, the Arctic Council was not prepared for the increased interest in its operations and their lack of readiness led to many misunderstandings about the council. Misunderstandings risked the status of the forum, which up to that point had been largely left alone to get on with its work.

Terry Fenge and Bernard Funston state in greater detail that criticism directed toward the Arctic Council in the mid to late 2000s was fuelled by misconceptions about "the Council's mandate, structure, procedures, operations, accomplishments/failing and future prospects" (Fenge and Funston 2015, 6). Members of the public thought the Arctic Council was more than it was and projected upon it a misconception that it was an international institution with further-reaching focus and authority than it was. As one former representative reflected, "people viewed the Arctic Council in the mid-2000s as the Arctic UN," which led to "great misunderstanding" (Former representative to the Arctic Council, 12 October 2016).

When the Arctic states considered how best to address these misunderstandings, one avenue they decided to use was mass media. When mass media is used, it is important to contextualize it, since, as S.A. Chunawalla warns, "mass media cannot be imagined without its cultural context" (2010, 6). What was the context in which the Arctic Council found itself after the 2007 flag-planting incident? How did its daily practices contribute to that context, and how did those practices and internal hierarchies or pecking orders influence both the way communication issues were addressed and the content of the messages the forum chose to disseminate?

In order to address the myriad misunderstandings that had arisen, the Arctic Council was obliged to upgrade its communications with the international community. It also needed to let the world know what projects it was involved in. A representative commented to me that, "the work that is being conducted is high, high quality, but the way it is being communicated is still lacking but being addressed. Definitely being addressed and improved" (Representative to the Arctic Council, 1 November 2017). A major impetus in this effort was to begin to engage the public using social media such as Twitter, which started in earnest under the Swedish chairmanship (2011–13) at the behest of the Swedish delegation. Communication through social media may be expressed through simple messages, but it is useful in conveying important facts about the Arctic and the Arctic Council to the public (Former Arctic Council chair, 2 September 2016).

This move to incorporate digital diplomacy has, as hoped, had a positive impact on dispelling misconceptions about the Arctic Council. Research suggests that social media is an effective avenue for digital diplomacy when it comes to targeting a diverse group of stakeholders, but this is the case only "if social media is used in an engaging way, using an appealing communication style that suits the media environment" (Strauß et al. 2015, 370). The Arctic Council has endeavoured to make its communication via Twitter attractive and accessible by, for example, providing images, offering links to reports, and using simple and straightforward explanations.

The Arctic Council's official Twitter account is an open account (viewable by anyone with no privacy settings on) and, as of 1 April 2018, it had twelve thousand followers. The following Tweets from the @ArcticCouncil account give a sampling of the Arctic Council's voice on social media (but due to copyright issues, the accompanying photos cannot be included).

[Tweet from 8 December 2017] From Working Group CAFF (@CAFF_Secretariat): beautiful educational toolkits for kids on

#Arctic #biodiversity – Life Linked to Tundra, Life Linked to
Spring, and Life Linked to Ponds. Check them out!

[Tweet from 6 December 2017] The #Arctic Council: A forum
for #peace and #cooperation (Joint statement from Ministers
for our 20th anniversary)

[Tweet from 4 December 2017] "Invasive alien species represent
a significant and rapidly emerging threat to #Arctic ecosystems
and inhabitants who depend upon these ecosystems for their
livelihoods and well-being." (Arctic Invasive Alien Species:
Strategy and Action Plan 2017)

[Tweet from 1 December 2017] Over millennia, #Arctic
#indigenous peoples' culinary traditions and #food culture
have nourished peoples, enriched communities, bound genera-
tions and embodied the very essence of #sustainability.

These examples were all accompanied by images that helped further communicate the work of the Council, attract attention to
the posts, and increase clicks through traffic to the Arctic Council
website via the Tweets.

DISCUSSING MILITARY MATTERS
IN THE ARCTIC COUNCIL

Efforts to introduce digital diplomacy were aided by the establishment of the permanent ACS and the digital Arctic Council
archives, which helped to streamline the information dissemination process. External communication challenges nevertheless
persist, specifically the continued misconception that the Arctic
Council should be discussing military matters. Across the board,
not a single representative to the Arctic Council interviewed for
this study, whether active or retired, conveyed any notion that the
Arctic Council was the place for these types of discussions; and
yet, suggestions to that effect continue to be made by some academics and researchers.

Heather A. Conley and Caroline Rohloff, authors of "The New Ice Curtain: Russia's Strategic Reach to the Arctic," a report of the Center for Strategic and International Studies (CSIS) Europe Program, for instance, recommend that "the eight Arctic Council states should begin to negotiate a non-binding political statement to serve as a 'Declaration on Military Conduct in the Arctic.'" Conley and Rohloff further suggest that the declaration statement should include "mandatory notification by every country 21 days in advance" for any major military exercise, which they define as consisting of more than 25,000 forces, and should include Arctic Council observer members (Conley and Rohloff 2015, xvi). The difficulty with suggestions of this nature, according to representatives to the Arctic Council, is that they risk complicating an already delicately balanced working relationship.

Many who have worked closely on regional Arctic issues acknowledge that there is a greater need to recognize that even though "security is not part of the mandate, there are security implications" resulting from what the Council does (Former representative to the Arctic Council, 2 September 2016). Efforts to foster cooperation, such as obtaining and maintaining the infrastructure needed to fulfil regional treaties, for instance, could have unintended security implications. One such treaty is the 2011 "Agreement on Cooperation in Aeronautical and Maritime Search and Rescue in the Arctic" (Arctic Council 2011a). However, even those who make such reminders point out that one must be "careful not to start talking security issues" within the Arctic Council context (Arctic state politician, 20 September 2016).

The issue of overlapping material assets – military and civil – involved in the implementation of Arctic Council agreements is a serious subject that has yet to be given an adequate response from the Arctic Council and its members. One example is the case of the US Coast Guard. Since it is part of the US Navy auxiliary forces, a US Coast Guard vessel could technically be designated a naval vessel if required (Retired Arctic Council chairperson, 7 June 2016), and this designation could in turn complicate relations with other Arctic states, mainly Russia (Pharand 1968). In contrast, the Canadian Coast Guard is a civilian organization, although it, too, works closely with the Canadian Armed Forces through aerial support for search and rescue work (Canadian Coast Guard 2018).

The issue of the vessels' classifications had already become an issue in 1967 when two US Coast Guard vessels – *Edisto* and *Eastwind* – attempted to pass through the Northern Sea Route/ Northeast Passage (Pharand 1968). The Soviet Union, like Russia now, claimed the Northern Sea Route was internal waters. The US vessels were in a standoff with Soviet authorities, who denied the vessels entry. The underpinning issue for the Soviet Union, according to legal scholar Donat Pharand, was that it was impossible for the Soviets to distinguish whether the vessels were transiting in their civilian capacity or as warships for the US Navy (Pharand 1968). Pharand argues that the Soviet authorities' interpretations of international law and innocent passage had "doubtful validity" (Pharand 1968, 935), but the fact that some vessels have dual identities and purposes can problematize discussions about search and rescue actions. Depending on the broader understanding of international relations dynamics among the Arctic states at the time an incident may occur, the dual identities of some coast guard vessels could delay emergency responses.

How can the potential security implications of having to implement a legally binding emergency agreement such as the Search and Rescue Agreement be resolved? The fact that the Arctic "is always a strategic area" calls into question Gorbachev's original "zone of peace" projection – the idea that the Arctic remain a peaceful area exempt from military tensions and disagreements. While "there was a time … when people thought the Arctic was a peaceful area," this is a misapprehension, given its geostrategic and geopolitical importance (Former representative to the Arctic Council, 2 September 2016). It is precisely because of the area's geostrategic and geopolitical importance that there was an intentional and explicit exclusion of military matters from the council's mandate.

The issue of the overlap between the intent of the treaties and the military hardware potentially used to fulfill treaty commitments needs to be addressed. Take the following hypothetical of an oil spill occurring in the Russian Arctic. Due to cooperation provisions in the Search and Rescue Agreement, council members need to request entry into the neighbouring states' sovereign waters before going in to help, but an offer of assistance to the affected party could hypothetically get mired in politics. Some of the main assets capable of helping with an oil spill are military assets. The Royal Danish Navy, for example, oversees search and rescue, as well as policing and patrolling the kingdom's coastlines; the Kingdom of Denmark does not have a separate coast guard (Hilde 2014, 161).

If the treaties that the member-states have signed do not stand up to a test because of concerns over the military nature of equipment used, the whole Arctic Council cooperation project could be jeopardized. There is currently a lack of political will from the Arctic Council member-states to talk directly about such issues.

One of the biggest fears from the outset of discussions to create the Arctic Council was the strong risk of alienating Russia if military issues were incorporated into the forum's work (Former Arctic Council negotiator, 29 August 2016; see also English 2013). This problem was highlighted when Canada pressed the issue of Russia's military conflict with Ukraine over the Crimea during its chairmanship (see chapter 4) (Exner-Pirot 2016b).

To include military issues in the forum is not seen as an effective way to maintain constructive Russian participation. One representative of a SAO noted, for example, that the permanent member-states agreed to the Arctic Council because of its "soft security focus [rather] than its hard security focus" (Representative to the Arctic Council, 10 May 2016). That interviewee went on to state that this soft security feature has helped the Arctic Council "sustain shock by not being nailed to a treaty," and clarified that it only takes one party to disagree with something for it not to happen (Representative to the Arctic Council, 10 May 2016). In the same vein, a retired Arctic Council chair also expressed a belief that keeping meetings away from hot-button topics like military and fisheries matters has enabled the Arctic Council to get into a solid working rhythm. This retired official further noted that, at least in the early years of the council's work, keeping hot-button issues away from the forum helped focus the council on developing a consistent working relationship with Russia and helped prevent a

shutdown when military and security tensions flared up (Retired
Arctic Council chairperson, 7 June 2016).

Other commentators expressed similar sentiments, apart from
some opinions expressed about Finland. Finland has been the one
Arctic state that has been consistent and open about its interest in
having the Arctic Council develop into a broad treaty-based international forum (Representative to the Arctic Council, 14 October
2016). Thus far, Finland has declared its position on the matter but
has strategically decided to not push the issue, given the lack of interest from other Arctic Council members (Representative to the Arctic
Council, 14 October 2016; Prime Minister's Office Finland 2013, 14).

Many have strong views on keeping the council focused on soft-
power subjects and away from those concerning security, particularly in light of Canada's handling of its 2013–15 chairmanship
during the Ukraine conflict. An interesting suggestion on this
issue was made by a Nordic Arctic research specialist, in order to
help open up discussions pertaining to the grey area of military-
related concerns involved in the implementation of treaties. The
researcher, in discussion with their colleagues, suggested that since
the member-states repeatedly suggest that there are other places
where these sorts of discussions can be held, such as the NATO-Russia Council (NRC), perhaps Arctic military discussions could be
redirected there (Group interview with three interviewees with
Arctic/Russian research specialists, 14 October 2016; see also North
Atlantic Treaty Organization 2017).

The NRC was established on 28 May 2002 by the Rome Declaration. According to the NRC website:

> The [NRC] is a mechanism for consultation, consensus-build-
> ing, cooperation, joint decision and joint action, in which the
> individual NATO member states and Russia work as equal part-
> ners on a wide spectrum of security issues of common interest
> … Hardly a day goes by without an NRC meeting at one level
> or another, leading to an unprecedented intensity of contacts
> and informal consultation in many different fields, conducted
> in a friendly and workmanlike atmosphere (NATO-Russia
> Council n.d.).

The potential of the NRC, however, has been cut short because of the Ukraine conflict. As a result of the conflict "the [NATO] Alliance suspended all practical cooperation between NATO and Russia including in the NRC" (North Atlantic Treaty Organization 2017). With the loss of the NRC, any mechanisms in place to discuss military issues with Russia, such as those in the Arctic region, have stopped working. It remains to be seen whether the avenue created by the NRC will open up again in the future.

In addition to the need to engage with Russia, the NATO member-states (Canada, the United States, the Kingdom of Denmark, Norway, and Iceland) have NATO meetings as an arena where they can discuss military matters among themselves and with allies. The Kingdom of Denmark, for example, sees NATO membership as the key to its defence and references Article 5, which is the article covering collective defence of NATO allies in its Arctic strategy document. At the same time, the Kingdom of Denmark also acknowledges that ultimately "the enforcement of sovereignty is fundamentally a responsibility of the Realm's central authorities" (Government of the Kingdom of Denmark 2011). This means that that the Kingdom of Denmark, like the other Arctic states that are NATO members and partner states, can, and do, benefit from collective security collaboration. However, the Arctic states also believe that it is important to be prepared to defend their own sovereignty, whether by military means or through diplomatic channels.

WORKING GROUP AWARENESS AND TRANSPARENCY

The other major external communication issue faced by the Arctic Council is the need to increase international awareness, access, and transparency about the work of the Arctic Council, particularly that of the Arctic Council working groups. As the discussion about funding in chapter 2 has illustrated, transparency is very hard to provide, when such a seemingly simple thing as calculating the cost of council projects is so complex. The issue of transparency relates to the problem of signalling. The Arctic Council is aware that it has communication issues when it comes to getting people outside the forum, even within the Arctic states, to understand basic facts about the Arctic region and the work of the forum. This is a challenge that the member-states and Permanent Participants are working on.

A further implication of the communication challenges is that the Arctic Council is sometimes accused of not being sufficiently focused on environmental work. According to one experienced working group member, the view that the Arctic Council has moved away from environmental work is enmeshed with other concerns (Representative to the Arctic Council, 13 October 2016). Since the increase in international interest in the Arctic Council resulting from the 2007 flag-planting incident and climate change, some delegates from the working groups have felt that the SAO meetings have become more focused on discussions about economics and sustainable development, and less on the environmental work. This perception of a shift in the forum's focus has been interpreted by some as a signal that it is trying to appeal to outside audiences. Some of those involved in the working groups are concerned that the shift in focus at the SAO meetings is feeding into the view that the economic side of the forum's mandate is now more important than the environmental.

Observer states and non-state actors are most exposed to the Arctic Council's work and agenda interests at the SAO and ministerial meetings. Generally, observers and the media get less exposure to the practices of daily cooperation unless, in the case of the observers, they choose to become involved with a specific project or working group. This means that if media coverage is more focused on the economic side of the Arctic Council's mandate, for instance, information concerning the economic work of the Arctic Council will be seen to have received more news coverage. The implication is that the high-calibre cooperative work of environmental research, reports, and clean-up projects is under-exposed.

The perception of some representations is that the change in the focus of SAO dialogues started around the time of the Danish chairmanship between 2009 and 2011 (Representative to the Arctic Council, 13 October 2016). This change came on the heels of the 2008 Ilulissat Declaration, which the Kingdom of Denmark played a strategic role in facilitating (Steinberg et al. 2015). As a result of this perceived shift, some members of working groups felt that their work, with the notable exception of the Sustainable Development Working Group (SDWG), had been sidelined as discussion topics in favour of more development-focused talk. According to a representative: "Basically … there are six working groups and only one of them is where the ministers of foreign affairs are represented and that's the SDWG. And the SDWG projects are understandable … they are talking about things that are kind of a priority … sustainable development and Indigenous communities and that kind of thing; traditional knowledge is really coming from there" (Representative to the Arctic Council, 13 October 2016). Since the work of the SDWG is arguably easier for representatives with a limited science background to understand, it is not hard to see why some representations may feel that SDWG topics get more attention from the SAOs; the SAOs probably feel that they are able to engage in more detailed discussions about SDWG work than about the projects of the other working groups.

An Arctic Athabaskan Council discussion paper, for example, observed that there was a need to improve the efficiency and effectiveness of the Arctic Council (Arctic Athabaskan Council 2007). One of this paper's key recommendations was that "the Arctic Council should make a concerted effort to avoid being perceived as a top-down enterprise controlled by policymakers and officials located in the national capitals" (Arctic Athabaskan Council 2007, 5). Unfortunately, the increased profile of the Arctic and the forum since the mid-2000s has served to aggravate this problem rather than encourage greater transparency and promotion of the internal work output and working dynamics.

Discussing the technical work generated by scientists can be problematic and not very user-friendly for laypersons unfamiliar with the intricacies of the research field. The language used by scientists can be opaque even to diplomats. According to Donna Marie Oglesby in her work on diplomatic language:

Scientists seeking to inform and influence politics on issues ranging from climate change to nuclear proliferation bring their own language conventions onto the diplomatic field.

> While suitably formal to diplomatic ears, scientific language insists on terminology with fixed meanings and greater specificity than that customarily used by diplomats. It challenges diplomatic representatives of political reality by insisting on scientifically determined objective knowledge of the real world then presumes to lock in only certain courses of action for international policy consideration (Oglesby 2016, 251).

Accessibility of information is not simply a matter of having data; it requires the skill to make that data understandable to any given audience without watering down the substance of the message in the process.

This communication issue is as much an internal challenge for the Arctic Council as it is an external one, as it relates to informing the world about Council activities. The Arctic Council is renowned for its high-quality environmental research, but with increased media attention on the forum and with the size of its meetings growing due to the increasing number of observers, ministers and representatives to the Arctic Council have become conscious that their words are being scrutinized more closely and may shy away from deep discussions of scientific work. As a result, some of those in the working groups are frustrated that their scientific work is being underrepresented in key meetings.

One representative, echoing sentiments of others at their approximate level, noted that it can be extremely difficult to discuss environmental research because they and many of their colleagues simply do not understand the details. It is not that they consider it unimportant – quite the opposite – but they struggle to keep up with the presentations made by members of the working groups and task forces. As this respondent elaborated:

> For member countries, especially in a forum where the delegates and the SAOs are career diplomats, the topics they raise and the things they prefer to discuss [are less scientific] ... this is a recurring issue. Some of the presentations by the working groups [at SAO meetings] are a bit too technical for some of the people in the room, including me. For people like me and

many of the delegates from the member countries, it's a challenge to discuss things that are not part of your background or daily work. Even so, we rely very much on the advice of the secretarial ministries on this particular issue ... It's not necessarily a problem that can't be handled, but I'm not sure it makes us discuss things like [technical work on environmental protection] less ... Even though we don't always understand what we talk about when we talk about the environmental protection ... the technical work that the working groups do on the issues is still very much active on the agenda (Representative to the Arctic Council, 1 November 2017).

As this viewpoint illustrates, there have been difficulties in articulating the environment-based research being done at the task force and working group levels within the Arctic Council. This can be attributed to two drivers: to a desire by the states to move the discussion toward economic development matters and to communications barriers arising from the technical nature of environmental research topics.

Time and again Arctic Council participants, politicians, and academics have emphasized the importance of the working groups. As is often stated about the forum, the "main work of the Arctic Council takes place within the working groups" (Weidemann 2014, 70). This value and expertise, however, needs more support to allow it to shine through and illustrate the overall substance of the forum's benefit for the Arctic and the world.

Two world-class researchers affiliated with the forum, who spent many years contributing to one such report, raised the very important concern about the extent to which reports generated by the Arctic Council are valued. Their concern is that little action is being taken to follow up on the recommendations of the authors in many of the high-quality reports and research generated by the Arctic Council's working groups and task forces. The frustrations of representatives and consultants stem from their bewilderment over the resources and the time used to create these reports if states are ignoring much of their work for political reasons and lack of comprehension of the science (Working group researchers, 26

October 2016). Similarly, another researcher affiliated with the Arctic Council reflected on the low level of action on reports generated by the council and lamented that the "working groups make high-level, professional documents, but ... few outside the Arctic ... know about it" (Representative to the Arctic Council, 15 September 2016).

This tendency has been noted by other researchers. Reporting on the effectiveness of the Arctic Council, Paula Kankannpää and Oran Young acknowledge, in their survey research with Arctic Council officials, that "the Arctic Council has been ineffective at following up the reports [of the working groups] with action" (Kankannpää and Young 2012, 7). The lack of effectiveness in following up on reports internally has very likely contributed to the forum's difficulties in articulating its work to international audiences. Issues regarding the forum's external communications have been coupled with internal communication issues.

According to an experienced working group representation, the problem of the three-way disconnect between the working groups, the SAOs, and ministers from the national governments reached its peak during the 2013 Kiruna ministerial meeting in Sweden, when an attempt was made to make presentation opportunities available for the working groups to display their projects. Although initially seen as a positive step in drawing attention to the working groups' outputs, the presentation time allocated for the working group displays in Kiruna overlapped with the time when the SAOs and ministers from the national governments were absent for a photo-op. As a result, top level officials and national government representatives had little opportunity to see the working groups' efforts. Furthermore, the presentations were set up in the Kiruna Mine (Arctic Council 2013d), and the press could not mingle among the presentations and presenters. The working groups ended up presenting to each other (Representative to the Arctic Council, 13 October 2016).

This issue of lack of communication opportunities at the executive level and with the media and international audiences, and the tensions it created for the working groups, was picked up on by the Canadian delegation during its 2013–15 chairmanship (Representative to the Arctic Council, 13 October 2016). Steps were taken to help bring international attention to the working groups, their expertise, and their outputs. For example, there were plans for a "one day showcase event in Ottawa the day before the ministerial meeting in Canada," which was intended to give the "working groups a chance to show work" (interview with a representative to the Arctic Council, 13 October 2016). Unfortunately, this event was cancelled in the fallout of the Crimea conflict. The intent behind the scheduling of the showcase, however, is a promising sign that the Arctic Council is trying to find avenues to better promote the work of the working groups to officials within the forum and to external audiences.

CONCLUSION

Overall, developing efforts to do more to bring international and high-level attention to the outputs of the working groups are a good sign that awareness is growing within the forum of the need to actively demonstrate its strengths to international audiences. This challenge remains an area where the Arctic Council needs to improve if the Arctic states and Permanent Participants want to ensure that the forum continues to be the central body for Arctic dialogue. Ultimately, the forum needs to develop consistent measures to ensure that it is cultivating the narrative about its work that it wants out in the public sphere. The likely implications of not prioritizing improvements in accurate communication are that non-Arctic actors will fill the void left by the Arctic Council with their own misconceptions and self-serving information about the region, the Arctic Council, and what they see as their role in both, without recourse.

7

The Observer Question

Clubs trying to maintain their status in the international arena often reach a point when their members question the role of the club and its structures, particularly when actors interested in or associated with the club recognize the benefits of club membership and try to obtain a role, and possibly increase their profile, within it. The heated debate in the United Nations over whether to reform the United Nations Security Council permanent membership is a prime example of a fixed club facing pressures to admit new members (e.g., Hund 2008; Schaefer 2017; Blum 2005; Weiss and Young 2005). For club members, finding ways to permit some level of club participation by non-core members can be beneficial; access to the skills and expertise of these actors can be useful. But it can be difficult to balance their involvement and with the need to maintain the exclusivity of core club membership; in this case it is a question of the permanency of Arctic states and Permanent Participants *versus* the conditional participation of observer members.

Like the Security Council, the Arctic Council is currently facing pressures to include outside actors. In principle, the Arctic states are not opposed to the involvement of non-Arctic actors in the Arctic Council. This is evidenced by the involvement of observers since the forum's inception, and in its predecessor, the Arctic Environmental Protection Strategy. However, the Arctic states are not unanimous about what exactly to do with observers (e.g., Steinberg and Dodds 2015).

Clubs require external recognition of their status to reinforce that status. Such recognition can come in the form of acts of recognition such as applications for membership and official statements of support for the club's work. Non-members (e.g., the European Union in case of the Arctic Council) and observers can further reinforce a club's status through contributions to club work, through lending their political support, expertise, and financial resources, and by providing access to data and equipment that could benefit the club's daily work (e.g., labs, scientific data, and satellite imagery). Recognizing that the benefits outweigh disadvantages, the Arctic states have in recent years been more open to the participation of observers in the Arctic Council.

As requests for observer status have proliferated, the Arctic states have become more diligent in clarifying the rules and procedures for observer admission and participation (Burke and Phelps Bondaroff 2019). In so doing, the Arctic states, through the Arctic Council, have once more reiterated their centrality in the leadership of the Arctic region. They have required non-Arctic actors to acknowledge this centrality as part of the cost of admission into the outer layer of the club's decision-making processes. This chapter highlights the divergences in opinions concerning observers in the Arctic Council and discusses two key points: first, general views of Arctic Council members toward observers; and second, delegates' opinions of different categoriesof observers.

These two themes emerged from interviews. Interviewees frequently noted that, in order to address the question of how to integrate observers into the forum, it was found necessary first to acknowledge the range of opinions about observer status that already exists, as well as the levels of scepticism held by Arctic state and Permanent Participant members. While some non-Arctic states have been granted observer membership, these states and other actors such as the EU are generally expected to "stay in their lane" as outlined in the manual for observers (Arctic Council 2013a) and the rules of procedure manual (Arctic Council 2013b). This stance is driven in part by the need to emphasize that observers will not have a status equal to that of the Arctic states or the Permanent Participants. As these outside actors push to have greater involvement in the Arctic Council and more applications for observer status are filed, the issue has come to a head, and the range of opinions about the place of observers has dominated discussion.

DIVERGING OPINIONS ON OBSERVERS

The representatives to the Arctic Council with whom I spoke indicated for the most part that the states they represented were favourably disposed toward the inclusion of observers in the forum, as long as value was added by their inclusion (Permanent Participant representative, 24 May 2016; Retired Arctic Council chairperson, 7 June 2016; Consultant to the Arctic Council, 14 June 2016; Representative to the Arctic Council, 21 June 2016; Representative to the Arctic Council, 7 September 2016; Representative to the Arctic Council, 13 October 2016; Representative to the Arctic Council, 8 September 2017). This being said, variations in the extent to which observers should be permitted to be involved in the forum were expressed.

Generally, the Canadians and Russians were seen to be more in favour of a smaller forum with a limited number of observers (Representative to the Arctic Council, 10 May 2016). As one individual reflected in an interview:

> In Canada our DNA is in more favour of a more closed operation. We were not that keen, historically, on this opening up [to observers] because we have been more proprietary in our approach; we have always been reluctant. This goes back to the establishment of the international science committee way back in the 1990s. The Europeans were always after us to involve more people and so on and so forth ... with a governing board which was limited to the states with the real estate in the Arctic. So that was always in our natural inclination, to be more closed, and the Russians were like that too. (No reference given, to protect the identity of the individual)

It makes sense that the two Arctic states that are geographically the largest would be the most cautious about opening Arctic dialogue and decision-making to outside actors. However, the perspective that the European Arctic states are more predisposed to observers than Canada and Russia is a bit too "black and white." A closer look reveals a more nuanced range of opinions regarding prospective observers.

At one end of the spectrum are the Nordic states who gave the impression that they are open to all types of observers. As one representative noted:

> Our basic policy is that we are open to new observers as long as they fulfil the formal criteria. We think it's even an asset to have many observers in the sense that many of the issues and challenges we are dealing with in the Arctic can't be solved by Arctic states alone … So we are very open to admit new observers … When it comes to non-state actors, as long as they have an Arctic focus and they can provide knowledge and insights, we are open to them as well. I think they have an important role to play. There are some that, for some people, are controversial organizations, like Greenpeace for example. For us, we have no problem to have them on board. We think it's good that they see what we are actually doing … but for others it might be a problem for different reasons. (No reference given, to protect the identity of the individual)

We cannot treat all the Nordic countries (Kingdom of Denmark, Finland, Iceland, Norway, and Sweden) as having a single unified position concerning the admission of observers, however. Sweden, for example, stands out as having the most open attitude toward new observer applicants. Sweden has been seen as the most supportive of Greenpeace's application within Arctic Council meetings – an application toward which the other Arctic states have been less receptive, or subtler in their support.

As one representative observed during the 2017 rejection of Greenpeace's application, in relation to determining what to look for in new observers:

> This is something that we've spent a lot of time on last time, before the Fairbanks ministerial [meeting] but we don't want

the Arctic Council to be too exclusive, but we don't want to Arctic Council to admit those without a clear Arctic profile ... Greenpeace has an Arctic profile. That's true ... First you need an Arctic profile and then you have to look at the candidates with the profile. [Many of the Arctic states'] experiences with Greenpeace are not the best. Very complicated history, so there were some countries opposing Greenpeace. (Representative to the Arctic Council, 8 September 2017)

When asked if any of the Arctic states were open to the admission of Greenpeace, this representative responded that, from their observation within the forum: "Sweden maybe, but we didn't vote for it ... it didn't come to a vote, because it's enough that one country blocks it ... Russia was very against it, Norway was against it" (Representative to the Arctic Council, 8 September 2017). As highlighted in this statement, Greenpeace is perhaps one of the most controversial observer applicants. This is largely due to its campaigning technique and legacy. The anti-sealing campaign, for instance, has had an influence on deterring interest for Greenpeace's application from Canada, the Inuit Circumpolar Council, and the Kingdom of Denmark. The anti-whaling campaigns have had a negative impact on Greenpeace's legacy in Iceland and Norway, and among various Indigenous peoples as well (Burke and Phelps Bondaroff 2019).

Greenpeace's involvement in many anti-development campaigns in other Arctic states has adversely affected relations with governments and influenced their views about the group's suitability as an observer from the perspective of those states. Campaigns of this nature include, but are not limited to: the anti-forestry campaign in Finland (e.g., Greenpeace International 2007; Finnish Forest Association 2017); anti-whaling campaign in Iceland (Greenpeace International 2014a; Greenpeace International 2009) and Norway (*New York Times* 1999; Greenpeace International 2014b; Laursen 2017); and anti-oil and gas development in Norway (Doyle and Solsvik 2018; Greenpeace International 2018; Fouche 2017), Russia (Stewart 2015; Greenpeace International 2017), and the United States (Pieters 2015; Greenpeace International 2015). As a result of such high-profile and active campaigning against these Arctic states, Greenpeace has developed strained relationships with their governments which contribute to the lack of success of their applications for observer membership to date.

Sweden is a bit of an exception in that it does not appear to have the same sort of reservations about Greenpeace. For Sweden "it's not a problem to have [Greenpeace] on board. Sweden thinks it's good that they [Greenpeace] see what we [the Arctic states] are actually doing" (Representative to the Arctic Council, 7 September 2016). Permanent Participants, on the other hand, are less inclined to bring Greenpeace into the forum. One Permanent Participant representative called Greenpeace "out of touch with nature" and "good liars [who] can't be trusted" (Permanent Participant representative, 25 May 2016).

Many representatives were sceptical about Greenpeace's suitability as an observer but were reluctant to elaborate on the record. While Greenpeace's application for observer status is just one example, it helps to illustrate the range of perception and agendas that exist in the Arctic, even among the Nordic states, who are perceived as more open to observer applicants but who have differing positions on the suitability of Greenpeace as an observer.

For its part, Greenpeace is aware of its image problem in most Arctic states, and with Indigenous peoples in the region, as a result of its past campaigning strategies, techniques, and outcomes. The legacies of the anti-seal hunt and the anti-whaling campaigns have plagued Greenpeace's hopes for acceptance into Arctic politics. The outcome of the anti-sealing campaign, for example, collapsed the sealing industry, with particularly devastating impacts on many northern Inuit communities and their economies. The legacy of Greenpeace's campaigning tactics, such as direct-action attacks targeted at sealers, who in the 1970s were primarily poorer people in society with little means of defending themselves against well-funded international attacks, still affects Greenpeace's campaigning efforts in the Arctic region, particularly among Indigenous peoples with whom they are now keen to work on their Arctic campaigns (Phelps Bondaroff and Burke 2014).

Greenpeace is aware of the double-edged legacy of the anti-sealing movement. On the one hand the collapse of the sealing industry is viewed as a major win in the organization's history and among its supporters, whose more than two decades of campaigning on the issue made it a high-profile international debate and defined public discourse about the industry in Europe. On the other hand, the techniques, future planning, and professionalism of the organization in the 1970s to the 1980s were quite different from the contemporary iteration of the NGO and have had a major impact on the organization's identity and current political opportunity structures. As one NGO representative reflected, "the professionalism of the [Greenpeace] organization was a lot lower back then" (NGO representative, 24 November 2016). The representative observed that as in the past, in the context of outreach in Greenland, for example, Greenpeace "sets back the relationship every time and makes the trust-building and the reconciliation a lot more difficult because – why should they trust us when we've already been there and tried to apologize and screwed up again?" (NGO representative, 24 November 2016).

In contrast, the two largest states in the region, Canada and Russia, have reputations for being more reluctant to admit new observers. During the formation of the forum in the late 1980s and early 1990s, Canada and Russia were concerned that observer status would become a problematic feature if it caused the Arctic Council to swell into something akin to the International Whaling Commission. The International Whaling Commission has eighty-seven member-governments, with landlocked countries such as Mongolia, Switzerland, and Austria as members, leading some to question why members who have no commercial interest in whaling are permitted a say in how the industry is managed (Keating 2014; International Whaling Commission n.d.).

It's really the Russians and the Canadians that are generally opposed to too much observer participation, and [make] threats or references to the whaling commission, which has [something] like 872 observers [*sic*] at every meeting. We don't want to go there. We want some observers but this is not

going to be a whaling commission. That was the main
thought. In the 80s, it would not just be a couple of environmental groups, like umbrella organizations, but there would
be Defender of Wildlife, there would be Greenpeace, Friends
of the Environment; and so the general sense [was] that this
[was] not exactly what we needed. (Retired Arctic Council
chairperson, 7 June 2016)

Russia and Canada remain the most cautious when it comes to
admitting new observers into the Arctic Council. They are open to
observers and see them as positive additions, as long as there is a
clear "value added" by their admission. It may be that Russia and
Canada are more selective than some of their counterparts about
how they calculate what constitutes "value added."

The United States has a somewhat mid-range attitude toward
the admission of observers. This reflects not only the country's relative psychological detachment from the Arctic but also the country's own status in international politics, which affords it a dis-
proportionate amount of leeway in comparison to most other
states. As a representative reflected on the US position: "The US
[position] has always been, 'Let's encourage more participants.'
That's kind of a broad stance we take. I can assume, if we want to
be cynical, that since we are big and strong and can get our way,
we can look more global" (no reference given to protect identity
of the representative).

Adding to the numbers of participants does not threaten the
status of the most powerful states in the same way as it might
other club members. The Arctic Council has always operated with
an implicit veto for Russia and the United States; the council was
able to form only because Russia was open to it, and the United
States entered with strict reservations on the agency that the
forum would be given (English 2013). Canada and the Nordic
states were aware that they needed the United States to participate
if they were to successfully engage with Russia, and this counterbalancing of great powers, coupled with the system maintenance
of the smaller Arctic states, continues implicitly.

CONCERNS ABOUT OBSERVERS

The concerns that representatives expressed about the growing number of observers focused on two main themes. First, what is the value added by including new observers? Second, could the inclusion of more observers have an adverse effect on Arctic Council proceedings? The issue of what value was added by observers became a point of increased attention within the forum, starting in 2013 with the publication of two documents, "Arctic Council Observer Manual for Subsidiary Bodies" (Arctic Council 2013a) and the "Arctic Council Rules of Procedure" (Arctic Council 2013b) document, soon to be followed by the 2015 "Addendum" to the manual (Arctic Council 2015c). By making these documents available, the Arctic states and Permanent Participants have begun to disseminate more explicit communications about what it is they want and expect from observers. Jian Yang argues that, through the establishment of, and adherence to, the rules of procedure and the observer manual, "the Arctic Council has reached its dual goals of restriction and exploitation, and effectively enhanced the Arctic importance in … global politics" (Yang 2016, 44).

Both the "Arctic Council Observer Manual for Subsidiary Bodies" and the "Arctic Council Rules of Procedure" lay out the conditions that all applicants must agree to prior to gaining observer status, including their explicit acceptance of the hierarchy of the membership categories. Both manuals state: "Decisions at all levels in the Arctic Council are the exclusive right and responsibility of the eight Arctic States with the involvement of the Permanent Participants. All decisions are taken by consensus of the Arctic States" (Arctic Council 2013a, 6; Arctic Council 2015c, 6). At the same time, however, the Arctic states and the Permanent Participants express interest in observer involvement. In so doing, they are explicit about what they see as the desired kinds of assets that observers can bring to the table: "expertise, competence and resources primarily in working group meetings and projects" (Arctic Council 2013a, 4). The idea appears to be that observer membership provides access to the forum through networking opportunities as well as opportunities to observe and assist the working groups.

Beyond accepting Arctic state and Permanent Participants' status in the forum's proceedings, would-be observers must also agree to additional limitations. Some of these limitations are practical. One prohibits observers from transferring their status to "another entity or organization to represent them at a meeting" (Arctic Council 2013a, 8; Arctic Council 2015c, 8). Two other limitations are very important for enforcing and supporting the status of the Arctic states in the forum: the first is that observer status, unlike Arctic state status or Permanent Participant status, is conditional. As the "Rules of Procedure" manual notes, observer status: "shall continue for such time as consensus exists among Ministers. Any observer that engages in activities which are at odds with the Council's Declaration or these Rules of Procedure shall have its status as an Observer suspended" (Arctic Council 2013b, 9).

The second limitation sets down some ground rules for the types of projects that observers may pursue. The Arctic states prohibit observers from undertaking projects in the Arctic if they do not have the backing of at least one Arctic state; that is, at least 50 percent of the funding for a project – and therefore support – must come from one or more of the Arctic states (Arctic Council 2013b, 9). By capping observers' ability to financially contribute greater amounts to projects than the Arctic states, and by making them answerable to the Arctic states and the Permanent Participants, the Arctic Council ensures that observer status remains subsidiary to that of club members. It should be noted that, in order to gain observer status, applicants must consent to these stipulations. These limitations do not stop observers from making valued contributions to the forum, but they certainly place boundaries on what observers can expect for those contributions.

Despite the development of rules of procedure for observer involvement in the forum, there are still internal debates within the Arctic Council about how to manage observer involvement and how to integrate observers more effectively (Representative to the Arctic Council, 10 May 2016; Representative to the Arctic Council, 21 June 2016). Again, one major concern raised by some Arctic states is a very practical matter (Representative to the Arctic Council, 10 May 2016; Representative to the Arctic Council, 21

June 2016; Former Arctic Council negotiator, 29 August 2016). As
the number of observers grows and applications increase, some
worry that the forum will lose its focus. As one academic who
researches Arctic relations notes regarding future expansion: "It'll
be interesting how that develops. Is there any roof on how many
members you take in? How many observers you might have? All
these kinds of things. That is also a question. How big can the Arctic Council become … before it loses sight if its purpose?" (An academic, 16 September 2016). These are serious questions that hark
back to the original concern of Canada and Russia during the
forum's creation. Representatives and academics from other parts
of the Arctic have also commented on the growing size of the
forum, but there is no clear answer to the question. It is, however,
a concern that the Arctic states and Permanent Participants are
aware of.

One reason that the club's core members – the Arctic states
and Permanent Participants – have expressed some concerns
with the growing size of the Arctic Council is that its expansion
is creating logistical problems at the most basic level of the
forum's work. This has always been a point of discussion, even
during the formation of the forum. As a retired representative
who was also part of the Arctic Council negotiation discussions
in the 1990s reflected:

> The Council Declaration provided for observers, but issues of
> how you got to be an observer and under what conditions you
> could observe, for non-governmental organizations, became a
> difficult one. It was eventually resolved, but there are still suspi-
> cions [about the process]. The other issue, which I think is on
> the way to being resolved, relates to observers from non-Arctic
> countries. With the issues of climate change coming to the
> fore, the number of countries interested in things Arctic has
> expanded greatly since the Arctic Council has been in opera-
> tion, and that has raised fears among members of the body
> becoming too large and unwieldy (Former Arctic Council
> negotiator, 29 August 2016).

Reservations about the size of the forum and its implications on cooperation still exist. Some delegates currently involved in the Arctic Council have commented on the fact that it is becoming difficult to hold meetings in Arctic venues and this is creating both physical and psychological separation between the forum and region.

Some feel that the forum's preoccupation with debating the role of observers and the swelling number of observers is already having an impact on the forum and its work. As one representative noted:

> The observer discussion has been going on for far too long ... It has become a distraction. But how we got here from there is that, when the Arctic Council started you could put three or four tables together and that was the entire Arctic Council – the states, the PPs and all the scientists – to the ministerial [meeting] in Norway where you had the entire conference hall that could seat five hundred people and it was full. (Representative to the Arctic Council, 10 May 2016)

Few venues within the North American Arctic region have the capacity to deal with such numbers at meetings. The ministerial meeting in Iqaluit, Canada, in 2015, for example, faced this issue. Though Iqaluit is the capital of Nunavut, it is not a large city. It is isolated from much of Canada, with no major highway or railway connecting it to Southern locations in the Canadian provinces, and as of 2016 it had a population of just over seven thousand, according to Statistics Canada (Statistics Canada 2016). Because of local capacity limitations, the American and Russian delegations had to fly in for the meeting and leave afterward since there was not enough space to accommodate them overnight (Morrow 2016).

How can the Arctic Council deal with the growing numbers of interested participants? It has yet to be determined whether the solution lies in measures such as enforcing caps on the number of representatives, limiting invitations to meetings, or holding meetings in southern parts of the Arctic states that offer larger venues and more capacious accommodations. However, in the view of some representatives, discussions about the observer issue are becoming an increasingly distracting administrative headache that is stealing time during high-level meetings from more important discussions such as those concerning the actual research and work of the forum.

Finally, opinions are divided about the quality of the contributions that environmental non-governmental organizations (ENGOs) make, particularly the World Wide Fund for Nature/ World Wildlife Fund (WWF). Currently the WWF has a generally very well received place as an active observer in the Arctic Council (Former representative to the Arctic Council, 11 May 2016; Representative to the Arctic Council, 21 June 2016; Representative to the Arctic Council, 14 November 2016). There are nevertheless dissenting voices that are more tempered in their reflections on the organization's participation. The WWF has been involved in the Arctic Council from the start, coming into the forum via the Arctic Environmental Protection Strategy when it was subsumed into the newly formed Arctic Council (Permanent Participant representative, 24 May 2016).

The WWF is highly praised by some for its research contributions, specifically the quality of its research. As one Permanent Participant representative stated: "They come over from the AEPS [Arctic Environmental Protection Strategy] and they have a global Arctic program, are very active in Arctic affairs, they put a lot of funding into research and they are very active in the Working Groups" (Permanent Participant Representative, 24 May 2016).

Not everyone gives as much credit to the WWF's approach to campaigning about Arctic issues, however. A different Permanent Participant representative, for example, expressed suspicion about WWF's science and their approach of monetizing nature in order to advocate for its protection (Permanent Participant representative, 25 May 2016). This stems in part from the broader context of ENGO involvement in campaigns such as those opposing sealing, whaling, and oil development, all of which have affected the lives of northern people, notably Indigenous communities. It is important to note that WWF does not campaign about oil development and has not advocated for the end of whaling or sealing among people in Arctic and sub-Arctic cultures. The criticism expressed is a reflection of the fact that ENGOs frequently claim that they are helpful in representing and working with Indigenous communities in international political discussions (e.g., Greenpeace and the "Save the Arctic" campaign) but have been met with mixed reception by Indigenous peoples and others (Representative to the Arctic Council, 14 November 2016). As a result of Greenpeace's 1970s–1980s legacy in the Arctic, ENGOs, regardless of their level of direct involvement in those campaigns, are often all painted with the same negative brush (also see Phelps Bondaroff and Burke, 2014). The WWF is no exception.

A reason that there are concerns with what ENGOs represent, particularly when they claim to help represent Indigenous interests, is that they have very different agendas than the Permanent Participants. As a retired diplomat elaborated:

This [in the Arctic Council] is where you might see even more participation from Indigenous and First Nations people. When they see NGOs with which they have had issues trying to be involved in this Arctic management, for example in the harvesting of nature resources ... there is real potential for confrontation there, I'm sorry to say. I think this is where they [Indigenous and First Nations] are not out-flagged, if you want, by the environmental NGOs that have totally different agendas. That is serious. That would get them more invested than ever in the process of the Arctic Council if they see that it will be taken over, to an extent, by environmental NGOs. (Former diplomat, 11 May 2016)

In the opinion of this retired diplomat, Permanent Participants are partly incentivized to be as involved as possible in the Arctic Council to act as a counterweight to the involvement of ENGOs, notably the WWF as the most active ENGO in the forum. Similar sentiments were expressed by a Permanent Participant representative who firmly stated: "They [ENGOs] are trying to impose their values on us and we're here to tell them no. And we have been fairly successful, particularly as until climate change, they didn't want to be where we are anyway" (Permanent Participant representative, 25 May 2016).

While many Permanent Participants and Arctic state representatives spoke highly of the WWF, some, such as a Permanent Participant representative with decades of advocacy experience, questioned its science and campaigning methods

> I think some of their science is actually suspect, myself. They have had something going for a while, the last ice area. They have scientists claim that this [*stands and shows me on a wall-mounted map*] is the last ice area and all the ice is gone. This will be the only area where ice hangs on and this place should be set aside as a refuge for polar bears and they had a thing on the go with Coca Cola to designate the areas [around the Northeast of Ellesmere Island and the Northwest of Greenland] because that is where all the polar bears will come to because it will be the last area where ice will be and it has to be protected … And how can they propose to speak that the polar bears will actually do that, go there? (Permanent Participant Representative, 25 May 2016)

> They [the WWF] also embarked upon a system where you basically monetize nature … We don't even begin to understand where they are coming from. It's so "anti" what we believe as Inuit. What's a bowhead whale worth? What's a culture worth? What's a language worth? Come on, let's get real here! There are some things to some people that you can't monetize. (Permanent Participant Representative, 25 May 2016)

It is important, therefore, not to take it for granted that everyone agrees with the high esteem accorded any actor within the Arctic Council and acknowledge the diverse perspectives that actors have and which have an impact on their status among club members.

Another issue is that, in the past, Arctic state representatives noted rumblings of dissatisfaction among observer states to the effect that they were ranked equal to ENGOs. Some felt that they should be giving a higher status of some sort.

> The problem created was the lumping together of observer countries and observer groups. Some of the observer countries are saying, "Look, I don't like to be sitting next to defenders of wildlife, or whatever. We should have a separate role as a country." And they do, in a way, but the Council is rather rigid in this. They have the eight countries, and we're the Arctic countries and we make our decisions, and you can have a voice and you can say things, but practically we're it and no we are not going to give more weight to representatives of Korea or China or something like that. They'll just [be] observers. (Retired Arctic Council chairperson, 7 June 2016)

This issue has largely been dealt with by the Arctic states, who made it very clear through the 2013 manual that all observers were going to be held to the same general standard of conduct and that the observer category was not going to be granted its own artificially imposed hierarchy. Any implicit status gained by observers and their representatives would have to be earned from individual actors and their representatives as they participate and contribute to the work of the Council.

CONCLUSION

Overall, the question of how and whether to incorporate observers into the Arctic Council has been a big focus for the club and its core membership. As the general views toward observer members indicate, while there are formal criteria to guide the assessment of observer applicants, there is no single stance on whom to admit and what to do with them once they obtain membership. The generally held opinion is that observers must add value, but what each Arctic state and Permanent Participant values is different.

While the observer states have expressed the view that there should be various levels of observer membership, the Arctic states and Permanent Participants are unwilling to give in to the pressure to create a formal hierarchy of observers just to satisfy the observer states. The debate is seen as a distraction by the categories of observers trying to elevate their positions within the club but forgetting, ultimately, that regardless of how they want to describe their observer status, among themselves they are just that, observers – not Arctic states and not Permanent Participants. That being the case, the inclusion of observers can be an asset for furthering the Arctic Council's work, but it is also a burden in some ways. In their push for greater participation in the forum, the observers are simultaneously creating physical and psychological distance between the Arctic's pre-eminent forum and the region and peoples it is trying to represent. This situation poses a challenge that will remain an ongoing subject for the Arctic Council in the years to come.

8

Coastal *versus* Non-Coastal States and the Pressure to Evolve

The issue of internal pecking orders and international status hierarchies in the Arctic Council is most clearly observable in the debate over the differentiation between coastal and non-coastal states within Arctic politics. International status hierarchies focus on states and how they are arranged, but such hierarchies are a reflection of more than states' comparative GDP or military capabilities; the process of establishing and maintaining them is more subtle and complex. The attribution of state placement in hierarchies reflects the reality that "between the possession of resources and the attribution of social value lies a vast province of social interaction, political contestation and symbolic construction" (Pouliot 2016b, 81).

The Arctic states recognize the implications for their mutual objectives in the region if they appear divided (see also Burke 2019). Any appearance of division could undermine the status of the Arctic states in Arctic cooperation as exemplified by the Arctic Council and leave them vulnerable to other actors claiming greater suitability for managing, at least, the common area of high seas in the Central Arctic Ocean. Nevertheless, internal divisions in the Arctic Council persist.

THE EMERGENCE OF THE ARCTIC FIVE

In international forums and organizations, "diplomacy is not just about a bunch of people of flesh and blood squaring off but also about the corporate entities represented at the table" (Pouliot

2016b, 75). Diplomats are more than mere pawns of states. Their ability to operate is often heavily influenced by the hierarchical standing of their states, which is itself affected by factors such as structural features that may be beyond their capacity to change. As Vincent Pouliot comments: "Multilateral diplomats do partake in this global epistemic debate over state markers of standing, but mostly at the margins ... At the level of diplomats themselves, though, such opportunities are [less frequent]" (Pouliot 2016b, 82).

At the same time, however, a state's ability to operate internationally is also conditional on its diplomatic envoys and their effectiveness. My interviewees noted the following characteristics as key to supporting diplomatic effectiveness: funding and access to resources; networks and their time to build upon them; the institutional memory within the diplomatic representation; and their representatives' individual employment histories. National areas of expertise also come into play, and can at times reflect a state's size or economic standing. This is not an exhaustive list of factors that can influence diplomatic effectiveness. Gender (e.g., Herman 1995; Rahman 2011; Neumann 2008; Aggestam and Towns 2018) and race (e.g., Blaschke 2016; Rosenfeld 1995; Quan 2004) are also acknowledged, but I focus here on the issues highlighted by practitioners.

According to Pouliot, the "principle of sovereign equality notwithstanding, in any multilateral setting, some state representatives weigh much more heavily than others" (2016b, 1). The Arctic states are diligent about projecting a united front to outside audiences and have been remarkably successful in doing so, using the Arctic Council and consensus practices to help demonstrate their unity. With the intention of sending a clear signal about Arctic solidarity to external audiences, the Arctic states even went so far as to adopt "One Arctic: Shared Opportunities, Challenges and Responsibilities" as the Arctic Council's slogan during the United States' 2015–17 chairmanship (U.S. Chairmanship of the Arctic Council n.d.). Nevertheless, between the representatives of the Arctic states and Indigenous peoples' organizations there are still pecking orders. And, as Pouliot reminds us, in multilateral diplomacy and international politics "there is not one international pecking order, relatively stable and immanent, but several of them, contested, changing and multifaceted" (2016b, 4).

The relative positioning of the Arctic Five and the non-coastal states illustrates one such pecking order. The Arctic Five have a reputation of banding together on Arctic maritime matters, arguing that they have the largest stake in any outcomes affecting maritime areas. They attracted particular attention for excluding others from negotiations and meetings, most notably in preparing the 2008 Ilulissat Declaration and at the 2010 meeting of the Arctic Five at Meech Lake in Canada (Steinberg et al. 2015, 1; English 2013, 1–2). Some representatives recommend this separation, noting that the inclusion of all eight states in maritime discussions can sometimes actually be detrimental to regional cooperation; it may slow down decision-making, on account of the need to include a larger number of opinions, including the voices of some countries not directly affected by the outcome of agreements.

The non-coastal states (Sweden, Finland, and Iceland) disagree with the view that the Arctic Five deserve elevated status within regional cooperation (e.g., Representative to the Arctic Council, 7 September 2016; Representative to the Arctic Council, 12 May 2016; Representative to the Arctic Council, 21 June 2016). Iceland has been the most outspoken about the problematic nature of the Arctic Five categorization and its own status as a coastal state (Dodds and Ingimundarson 2012). Iceland's opposition to the Arctic Five, however, has received mixed responses from the other countries, who express skepticism about Iceland's argument: "Iceland is probably the most open of the Arctic states to criticize the Arctic Five form. You never know, if they could somehow join the club, [Iceland] might switch views" (Representative to the Arctic Council, 7 September 2016). But Iceland is not likely to change its position any time soon. A driving force behind its opposition to the Arctic Five is its disagreement with what it sees as the questionable use of the Exclusive Economic Zone (EEZ) adjacent to the Arctic's high seas as a defining factor for status as an Arctic coastal states – a point about which the Government of Iceland is passionate (Representative to the Arctic Council, 21 June 2016).

The status of the Arctic Five took shape gradually in the early years after the formation of the Arctic Council, with Canada and Russia being its most vocal supporters (e.g. English 2013, 1–2). It was the Kingdom of Denmark that proposed that the five Arctic coastal states could be more effective in dealing with maritime misunderstandings; namely, it saw the merits of having the coastal states band together to create the Ilulissat Declaration in 2008. The Ilulissat Declaration was a response to the rapidly growing interest in the Arctic, and the misconceptions that dominated discourse about the region at the time (Steinberg et al. 2015, 9–12).

While the existence of the Arctic Five is controversial, the Kingdom of Denmark's initiative and the support for it from the other coastal Arctic states is illustrative of the need to sometimes step outside standard conventions of regional dialogue and the Arctic Council to deal with immediate problems. Of course, it is important to acknowledge that deviations from norms are risky endeavours in any diplomatic context (see chapter 4), but if actors are successful in their deviation then they can create new patterns of interaction within the diplomatic community.

Pouliot notes that successful diplomats who have mastered their diplomatic environment understand how to navigate the social rules and are open to risking deviations from them:

> Practical mastery does not reduce [actors] to strictly following social standards. Sometimes this is the case, but in other situations it is deviance that actually wins the day … Deviations from established ways of doing things are often deemed incompetent by the community and, as a result, they fail to create new patterns. The outcome depends on a complicated and contingent politics within the community of practice, in which competent players manage to impose certain practices over others. (Pouliot 2016b, 57–8)

The explicit emergence of the Arctic Five with the Ilulissat Declaration is a clear example of such deviations from the established way of cooperating in the Arctic region. The deviation from the use of the Arctic Council to the use of the Arctic Five does not necessarily mean undermining cooperation through the Arctic Council. The use of Arctic Five has, however, highlighted the pecking order of coastal versus non-coastal states and dispelled the notion that all eight Arctic states have equal status.

The Arctic Five have been useful in dealing with the unanticipated swell in interest in the Arctic region and in clarifying misunderstandings about national jurisdictions and the application of the law of the sea. The group does recognize that the use of the Arctic Five could undermine their broader regional agendas, however. Deviating toward discussing Arctic maritime matters exclusively among the Arctic Five would mean encroaching upon some matters on which they have already agreed to cooperate within the Arctic Council. Further deviations from social norms, if managed poorly, could undermine not just the legitimacy of the Arctic Five, but also the Arctic Council itself. In the end, the debate among the eight Arctic states about the use of the Arctic Five boils down to this point: "If you [took] out all the ocean-related issues from the Arctic Council there would be nothing left for the Arctic Council to discuss, or very little" (Representative to the Arctic Council, 7 September 2016).

As one representative who was involved in the creation of the Ilulissat Declaration reflected:

> The thinking at the time was that the Arctic Five was meant to be a one-off for that purpose. It wasn't established as a cooperation [venue] besides the Arctic Council, or in conflict, or competition with the Arctic Council. Everybody agreed at the time that the Arctic Council was the regional organization relevant for the region, but there was a need at the time for something that was only relevant to five of the members. It wasn't an attempt to establish a new type of cooperation. (Former representative to the Arctic Council, 12 October 2017)

Since the Ilulissat Declaration, and the subsequent 2010 meeting at Meech Lake, the Arctic Five have become subtler in demonstrating their status within Arctic diplomacy, although the status of and influence of the Arctic Five are still pervasive. This is illustrated by those actors who are currently proposing moving the Arctic Council toward a more policy-making, rather than a policy-shaping body and how such a proposal is received within regional cooperation.

PRESSURES FOR CHANGE IN ARCTIC GOVERNANCE

As interest in the Arctic continues to grow, the Arctic states face pressure to do more to secure their status at the top of the regional and international hierarchy as the prime movers of Arctic cooperation. One of the strongest pressures is for the Arctic Council to move away from its current format and to become a treaty-based organization. Finland is the Arctic state that has most openly expressed its support for such an effort. Finland's 2013 Arctic strategy document stated: "The Arctic Council's institutional role has been growing following the establishment of a permanent secretariat, the conclusion of binding international agreements and the extension of the Council's agenda. Finland supports the continuation of this development and the recognition of the Arctic Council as a treaty-based international organization" (Prime Minister's Office, Finland 2013, 14).

Within the Arctic Council it is well known that Finland would prefer the council to become part of a system with a treaty at its core and as a result, have greater policy-making authority. But for its part, Finland and its representatives are careful to not push their views on the matter (Representative to the Arctic Council, 14 October 2016). Finland is keenly aware that it has limited internal support within the Arctic Council for its position. The Arctic Five are concerned about the implications that such changes would have on their long-term interests. The fact that Finland resists pushing the issue indicates both Finland's status within the forum and the lack of support for the notion within the Arctic Council.

Canada and Russia are the most openly cautious in their approaches to change. As the two states with the most territory and largest maritime zone in the Arctic region, they would be the states that experienced the most direct impact of any changes to the region's governance practices.

The United States has also been observed broaching the subject of the Arctic Council's becoming a legally binding institution, notably during its 2015–17 chairmanship. This position stands in stark contrast to its stance at the time when the forum was being created in the early to mid-1990s (Torbjørn 2012, 149). The United States, however, is also known for not committing to initiatives in whose creation it took a lead role (e.g., League of Nations, United Nations Convention on the Law of the Seas, UNCLOS) (Torbjørn 2012, 149). It has also had an unclear relationship with the Arctic Five; U.S. Secretary of State Hillary Clinton was noted in 2010 as expressing the opinion that the Arctic Five might create "new divisions" (English 2013, 1–2). Clinton's concern was that the Arctic Five would create divisions among the Arctic states and between the Arctic Five and the Indigenous peoples of the region. At the same time, the United States is at the top of the international hierarchy in international politics, a position that is not affected by its participation in the Arctic Five. This means that the United States is uniquely placed compared to the other members of the Arctic Council and the Arctic Five; whether in relation to the Arctic Five or the Arctic Eight, the status of the United States within the pecking order among the Arctic states is secure for the time being.

Permanent Participants are leery of suggestions for structural change, in part because of their own status positions within the forum and the limited capacity of their representatives to have any impact on the consensus processes. The participation of Indigenous organizations at the Arctic Council is a unique aspect of the Council's format and practices, and their involvement in the forum has been instrumental in maintaining the forum's legitimacy. Interestingly, though, the Permanent Participants are strangely placed in the hierarchy; their representatives have an unclear standing within the diplomatic pecking order.

On the one hand, the involvement of the Indigenous peoples' organizations as Permanent Participants demonstrates an effort on the part of states, particularly Canada, which has been a very vocal advocate for their involvement in the Arctic Council, to break with its colonial past. This colonial past saw Indigenous peoples marginalized in the politics of their homelands. While efforts to address this legacy are politically sensitive, the permanent inclusion of Indigenous organizations in the Arctic Council provides Indigenous peoples with the security to speak their minds without concern that they will be excluded from meetings or expelled from the forum. Indigenous representatives are free to speak with a strong voice. On the other hand, the effort to break from the colonial past is complicated by the reality that the Permanent Participants lack a formal voice in consensus decision-making, and the colonial legacy and experiences of Indigenous peoples vary among the groups and the Arctic states.

The Permanent Participants derive their power in the Arctic mainly from the art of persuasion and the force of public shaming rather than from any formal power allotted to them through the structure of the Arctic Council. Indigenous organizations are aware that they are especially vulnerable to changes to the forum, notably on matters that move away from traditional knowledge toward science-based research or general foreign policy concerns. While changes in the structure of the Arctic Council could lend them more authority, these changes could undermine their power as well. Since the latter is at far greater risk until more concrete proposals for change are available for review and debate, the Permanent Participants generally favour the status quo.

When it comes to foreign policy matters, the influence of Indigenous peoples can be observed filtering into Arctic Council politics at the domestic level. The most interesting example is the Kingdom of Denmark. In the kingdom's delegation, the context of Indigenous representation is more complex than in some other states. Greenland's existence within the Kingdom of Denmark provided the substantiation for Denmark to be considered an Arctic state, and yet Greenland is a former Danish colony that is now a semi-autonomous part of that kingdom. In January 1979 Greenland held a referendum that formally began its process toward independence. According to the Naalakkersuisut/Government of Greenland website, the referendum resulted in 63 per cent of the electorate voting in favour of home rule on 1 May 1979. Home rule began the process of decentralizing powers to govern local affairs from the Danish government to local governments (Foighel 1979).

The 1979 referendum was followed on 21 June 2009 by the Act on Greenland Self-Government, which extended the powers enacted in the Home Rule Act. According to the Greenlandic government:

> Through the Home Rule and Self-Government Acts Greenland has the right to elect its own parliament and government, the latter having sovereignty and administration over the areas mentioned in the Self-Government Act such as education, health, fisheries, environment and climate. Some of the achievements of the Self-Government Act were the recognition of Kalaallit (Greenlanders) as people, in international law, the opportunity for Greenland to become an independent state, as well as the opportunity to take on the jurisdiction of more areas (such as natural resources and justice affairs). (Naalakkersu- isut/Government of Greenland n.d.)

The Greenlandic population consists predominantly of Inuit people and they have direct representation in the Arctic Council within the Danish delegation.

Greenland's emerging autonomy has at times led to internal disputes within the Danish delegation. Here is an example:

> In 2013 Greenland's Premier, Aleqa Hammond, boycotted the Arctic Council's meeting between the top-level Arctic Council officials in Kiruna, Sweden. Premier Hammond's reasons for protesting the meeting included the Kingdom of Denmark's delegation structure. Denmark represents the Kingdom within meetings, which means that the representatives of Greenland and the Faroe Islands sit behind Denmark's top official, thereby signalling their subordinate status to Denmark … Since 2013, representatives for Greenland have commented on improvements with the Kingdom's approach toward Arctic Council meetings. Now there is more internal communication and pre-meeting discussion and debate between the three parts of the Kingdom on the Kingdom's agenda in preparation for Arctic Council meetings. The Kingdom has an agenda that reflects a more united approach as a result. (Burke 2017a)

Greenlandic representation in the kingdom's delegation and in the Arctic Council agenda may now reflect greater parity, but the Greenlandic people are also represented by the Inuit Circumpolar Council (ICC) through the ICC Greenland branch of the organization. This unique position of explicit double representation sometimes puts them in situations of conflict of interest. When it comes to issues related to the Greenlandic people, the ICC and the Greenlandic government do not always have the same position or agenda. Questions about development opportunities are a clear example (Government representative in an Arctic state, 14 September 2016).

Canada also has cultivated an image, both domestically and on the international stage, as a champion of Indigenous inclusion in the Arctic Council, and consequently puts a large amount of political and public support behind maintaining a strong Indigenous presence in the forum. Canada's selection of Leona Aglukkaq, the first Inuk to chair the Arctic Council, is evidence of its commitment that Indigenous voices are essential to regional dialogue (CBC News 2013). Representatives for Canada have expressed the view that Canada is firm that any proposed changes to the Arctic Council cannot come at the expense of representation of the Permanent Participants (e.g., Representative in the Arctic Council, 12 May 2016). Since Indigenous representatives operate under different conditions than representatives of state members of the council, however, and as their groups operate as minorities within their states (except in Greenland), it is quite difficult to place them and their organisations within the forum's pecking order, relative to the state members and their representatives.

Overall, the idea of reforming the Arctic Council has stalled. While Finland supported the general principle, the Arctic coastal states, particularly Canada and Russia, have little interest in such a project. In addition, unless there are explicit principles to protect the status of the Permanent Participants in any proposed agreement, then Indigenous peoples are unlikely to support the idea either. While Permanent Participants may lack a formal say in the consensus decision-making, they play a vital role in the legitimization of the Arctic Council. A decision to change the forum without their expressed approval would create major issues both for the status of a revised Arctic Council and for the legitimacy of its new format.

THE ARCTIC FIVE AS A TOOL
IN REGIONAL UNITY AND STATUS MAINTENANCE

Given the widespread resistance to substantial forum restructuring, the Arctic Five have taken on a more central role in certain aspects of Arctic politics, particularly as these states push back against external proposals for high seas management. The Crimea dispute and Canada's management of it while chair undermined the notion of the united Arctic Five and flamed ideas of fractioned unity and discontent. This was especially problematic because the Arctic Five have been referred to by some politicians as "being necessary at a time when the renewed interest in the Arctic region [has been] depicted as a race and a scramble for natural resources" (Pedersen 2012, 150). By addressing certain issues as the Arctic Five, those countries are sending a signal to other states that gaining access to the Arctic region and determining how its resources are managed are Arctic matters that should stay within the purview of the Arctic states. The continued use of the Arctic Five approach further consolidates an elevated status for the coastal states over the other members within the Arctic Council and in regional cooperation in general.

The benefits of the use of the Arctic Five may outweigh the drawbacks, at least in the short term. One representative from a non-coastal Arctic state cautioned, however, that use of that grouping could have long-term implications for regional solidarity and the success of its model of cooperation:

> Now we have another issue, that is trying to see if we could reach an agreement on marine-protected areas ... in the seas beyond national jurisdiction. I wouldn't rule out the possibility that there will be a tendency to [have] these issues on an [Arctic Five] basis, but we are strongly against that. I think actually that, apart from Finland, for obvious reasons, there are others, including coastal states who are not very happy – the US, for example ... So we are not alone. The main reason is that we

have an important organization that is functioning well. It's unique. We shouldn't destroy that. (Representative to the Arctic Council, 7 September 2016)

Despite this concern, the Arctic Five have led discussions about the conservation and sustainable use of the Arctic's high seas, focusing on a regional fisheries management agreement, matters that lie beyond the Arctic Council's mandate.

The issue of high seas overfishing is a serious problem, but it also presents an opportunity for the Arctic states and the Arctic Five. By leading the effort to address governance and regulatory gaps in the Arctic's high seas, the Arctic Five can further demonstrate their status. In so doing, they would be countering pressures from the United Nations open-ended informal working group assigned to study the conservation and sustainable use of marine biological diversity beyond areas of national jurisdiction (BBNJ) (e.g., Oceans & Law of the Sea n.d.; IISD 2017). The BBNJ is discussing widespread change for high seas governance. Concerns have been raised that such widespread change in high seas governance in the Arctic could affect the Arctic in ways undesirable to the interests of the Arctic states (IISD, 2015).

Plans for an Arctic high seas fisheries agreement emerged in earnest in the media in 2014 (*Globe and Mail* 2014). In a multilayered approach, the Arctic Five spearheaded an initiative to develop a regional agreement to protect the Arctic's high seas. The Arctic Five came together first as a group, and later with four other states (Iceland, China, Japan, and South Korea) and a pan-state actor, the European Union (EU), to form what has been called the A5 + 5 (Min 2017). Their decision to form the A5 + 5 to discuss Arctic high seas fisheries management correlates with the start date of the BBNJ negotiations.

Internally among the eight Arctic states, the Arctic Five have demonstrated that they have learned from Iceland's argumentative reaction to their collective exclusion of it from the Arctic Five (Dodds and Ingimundarson 2012). The Arctic Five have acknowledged Iceland for its strengths and capacity within the international fishing industry and that country has been included in the agreement negotiations on fisheries management of the Arctic high seas. In addition, the Arctic Five learned from Indigenous protests against their exclusion from the Ilulissat Declaration negotiations and the meeting at Meech Lake (English 2013, 1–5). This time around, Inuit peoples were consulted in the negotiations with "Inuit from Canada, Greenland, the Russian region of Chukotka and Alaska represented by the Inuit Circumpolar Council," although they were not technically considered part of the + 5 group (Sevunts 2017).

Of these +5 negotiation participant members, Iceland (as previously mentioned), Korea, and Japan have expressed reservations about proposed international changes to high seas governance, particularly with regard to fisheries (Wright et al. 2016, 37–8), whereas the EU and China are seen as more favourably inclined toward a legally binding instrument to deal with high seas governance (Wright et al. 2016, 30). What is clear is that all the +5 agreement participants are among the most vocal actors throughout the discussion about whether a new international legally binding agreement on high seas management should be reached. To this end, the Arctic Five have sought to create an agreement based on a critical mass of states that dominate the international fisheries industry.

Together the A5 + 5 started negotiations for a legally binding agreement to manage the research and use of the fish stocks in the Central Arctic. The Arctic Five are leading these negotiations with the aim of researching fisheries issues and imposing a temporary moratorium on Arctic fishing in response to mounting international efforts to exert authority in the region (*Canadian Press* 2014). The first move was a declaration by the Arctic Five in Oslo on 16 July 2015 for the prevention of "unregulated commercial fishing in high seas portions of the central Arctic Ocean" (U.S. Department of State 2015). The big issue highlighted in the meeting was that there is "limited scientific knowledge about marine resources" in the Arctic and that fishing without a good understanding of an ecosystem's capacity to sustain an industry would unwisely violate the precautionary principle (U.S. Department of State 2015).

Following from the July 2015 declaration of the Arctic Five, further collaboration was ear-marked, which subsequently led to negotiations for a treaty to regulate commercial fishing in the Arctic's high seas between the A5 and the 5 other states/pan-state actors in an area greater than 2.5 million square kilometres (U.S. Department of State 2017). The ten negotiating parties met again in Iqaluit, Canada, on 6–8 July 2016 to continue negotiations (Zerehi 2016; Rogers 2016). By acting parallel to the Arctic Council, but technically not in it, the A5 + 5, have endeavoured to keep core Arctic issues within the purview of the Arctic coastal states, while at the same time protecting the integrity of the Arctic Council's existing mandate and demonstrating a willingness to work with a key, but limited number of non-Arctic states.

The new legally binding international accord, the Agreement to Prevent Unregulated High Seas Fisheries in the Central Arctic Ocean, was announced in 2017. It will cover "an area that is roughly 2.8 million square kilometers in size, roughly the size of the Mediterranean Sea" (U.S. Department of State 2017). The agreement was reached after five rounds of negotiations, and it stresses a precautionary approach to regional fisheries management.

According to the European Union statement upon the completion of the negotiation surrounding the agreement: "The agreement envisions the creation of one or more regional fisheries management organisations or arrangements for the Central Arctic Ocean, to ensure that any future fishing is carried out sustainably" (European Union Science Hub 2017). While this is a major step toward finalizing a regional fisheries agreement lead by the A5, it is not a done deal. According to the U.S. State Department's statement on the agreement: "Before the Agreement will be open for signature, the delegations must first undertake a legal and technical review of its provisions, which will occur in the near future, and prepare the texts in the other languages in which it will be signed. During that time, delegations will also seek final approval within their respective governments to sign the Agreement" (U.S. Department of State 2017). As such, the agreement is still a few very important steps away from being formalized, the last of which being compliance with the agreement. Following the ratification of the treaty comes the most difficult part; adhering to the agreement.

Ultimately, however, by keeping the agreement negotiations localized to the needs and conditions of the Arctic region, the negotiations were more manageable in scale. As Glen Wright, Julien Rochette, Elisabeth Druel, and Kristina Gjerde state: "The regional approach to marine environmental protection can increase the likelihood of political consensus among parties as they may share a similar history, culture and interests in the region, and can provide an appropriate scale for the implementation of an ecosystem approach to conservation" (Wright et al. 2016, 18).

What is more, by taking the stakeholder approach with the leading fisheries industry states and pan-state actors, the Arctic Five have taken care to ensure that all major stakeholders were involved in the process, thereby preventing industry leaders from later circumventing the agreement by claiming they had been excluded from the process. The A5 + 5 have reached a draft agreement, and if the Arctic Five can manage to get it successfully adopted and implemented in the coming years, then this will constitute a major success that would reinforce the status of the coastal states, which was only possible through their unity. This agreement could also have the possible effect of decreasing the immediate interest for regional maritime governance change coming from other avenues, such as the BBNJ.

The A5 + 5 format is an implicit acknowledgement that the Arctic states are trying to limit non-Arctic coastal state input on Arctic maritime governance, but it also illustrates that inclusion is determined by the specific states whose competencies warrant their participation in negotiations. The A5 + 5 negotiations demonstrate practical mastery on the part of the Arctic Five as they work to protect their states' interests and maintain the integrity of the Arctic Council's mandate by refraining from pushing issues for discussion in that forum that go beyond its mandate. It also illustrates that the A5 insist on a leadership and central position for themselves in the process of jurisdictional development over the Central Arctic Ocean. By using the A5 + 5 to develop a regional fisheries management agreement, they have shown leadership in high seas stewardship before the process of regional management could potentially be co-opted by outside actors.

CONCLUSION

Overall, pecking orders within diplomatic environments can play a vital role in how proposals for change are received and the way actors at the top of those pecking orders can behave. Determining both an actor's relative position within pecking orders and areas of influence, however, is easier to approximate when assessing traditional actors of equal legal status in a given diplomatic environment. Context is key. The Arctic Five have relatively higher status in Arctic maritime discussions because they are the Arctic states with maritime boundaries in the Arctic Ocean, and as such have legal rights and developed competencies to manage these boundaries. That does not imply that the non-coastal Arctic states have nothing to add to maritime discussions but, depending on the context, the use of the Arctic Five alongside Arctic Council cooperation can be a strategic move that supports all Arctic states. Using the Arctic Five to deal with specific issues that lie outside the Arctic Council's mandate, for example, can help complement the Arctic states' status as regional leaders, preserve the Arctic Council's focus on areas within its mandate, and prevent the Arctic Five from being perceived as an alternative to the Arctic Council and thereby challenging the club's status.

When non-traditional actors in international politics such as Permanent Participants in the Arctic Council are considered, it is much more difficult to decipher their status relative to the other permanent forum members – the Arctic states. Similarly, insufficient data was collected during the fieldwork for this book to adequately access the relative pecking orders of Permanent Participants relative to each other within the Arctic Council, either. This is an area where much more work would be required.

Regardless, the underpinning promotion of the Arctic Council as a unique body thanks to its involvement of Indigenous peoples empowers the Permanent Participants in any kind of discussion regarding the evolution of the forum. As a result, their status within the internal pecking order may be difficult to determine, but the idea that they have status in it that is essential to the club's continued status in international politics is acknowledged and accounted for in decision-making.

Conclusion

At the heart of why the Crimea conflict has not derailed the Arctic Council is the recognition by regional representatives and actors that the outward projection of unity is central to their ability to address internal challenges in a manner that best meets their shared needs and reflects the limits of their willingness to compromise as well as helping resist external pressures from outside their core group in order to retain maximum decision-making power over their homelands and the waters adjacent to them.

Furthermore, the centrality and status of Russia in the Arctic Council project is repeatedly illustrated through the nature of, and approaches toward, internal and external challenges that the Arctic Council faces (for the clearest example see chapter 5). This is not to say that the Crimea conflict and Canada's handling of it did not threaten the club, because it did; but the clear reaction of the other Arctic states and their representatives (see chapter 4) to Canada, in refusing to encourage its stance against Russia within the forum while it acted as chair, emphasized the delicate diplomatic situation that arose and the core actors' awareness of the profound risks that alienating Russia would have on club unity.

The other states and the Permanent Participants appeared to take the approach of waiting out the clock until the forum's structures provided a natural and dignified conclusion to the Canadian control of the chair position, thereby depriving the situation of oxygen and stopping the fire from spreading within their forum and destroying the foundation of its networks and diplomatic goodwill. Rising external interest, pressures for access, and the creeping of outside agendas into the region incentivized the re-orientation of attitude and focus on the part of core club members during and after the Crimea conflict, to protect the council's status, the unity it represents, and the symbolic authority that it infuses into ideas of national state sovereignty and regional control.

As Part One of this book illustrated, the ways in which the Arctic Council was formed and has evolved since its creation in 1996 reflect the internal status of member-states and their relative ranking in pecking orders internal to the forum. The Arctic states and Permanent Participants face a number of challenges within the Arctic Council, which representatives to the forum highlighted in my fieldwork interviews. These challenges, particularly funding (chapter 2), have far-reaching implications on cooperation in the region. The challenges emphasize the complexity of regional cooperation and illustrate the role of status and pecking orders on how decisions are being made.

Pecking orders vary according to the topic of discussion or area of expertise (e.g., chapter 3, Institutional Memory), and they exist among the member-states and organizations, and individual representatives as well. Maintaining unity among the Arctic states and Permanent Participants is the biggest overall internal challenge to face the Arctic Council, but unity is a necessity, as it is the Arctic Council's main source of strength. Pecking orders and the relative status of members affect the capacity of the Arctic Council to project unity when national interests of certain states can threaten cooperation (chapter 4), but efforts to maintain unity also have the capacity to bolster the interests of actors in ways such as encouraging Russians and other non-English first language speakers to cooperate more fully (chapter 5). Regardless, unity is an empowering tool that makes the Arctic Council work as a club with legitimacy to operate. As Part Two of this book explored, unity also makes it easier for the Arctic states to cope with non-Arctic interests in both the Arctic Council and the Arctic region.

Part Two consisted of a discussion of the Arctic Council's management of its status in the broader international political arena.

More specifically, it addressed several challenges: the need to communicate effectively about the club and the Arctic region to dispel widespread misinformation in perceptions of them (chapter 6); to manage the interest and participation in the club by non-Arctic actors (chapter 7), and to withstand the pressures to change the forum's structures to accommodate the interests of additional actors (chapter 8). Overall, Part Two emphasized that the club has a status in international politics as the pre-eminent regional forum. If it is to maintain and reinforce that status, the forum and its core members must meet certain expectations and pressures from actors outside the region as to how Arctic leadership will manifest and evolve going forward.

As this book has emphasized, status is not static. The fluidity of status is compounded in the Arctic region by jurisdictional limitations; the Arctic states do not have absolute jurisdiction over the Arctic region. The high seas in the central Arctic Ocean are global commons (chapter 8), and the Arctic states lack the authority to prohibit access and use of the high seas of the central Arctic Ocean. That being the case, the need for international support for the status of the Arctic Council and Arctic states in regional decision-making is even more essential.

The overarching point is that clubs cannot exist in complete isolation from external influences and political events, regardless of how hard they may try. As the effects of the 2014 Ukraine conflict and the growing international interest in the Arctic region demonstrate, pressures and challenges from internal and external sources will make continued demands on club diplomacy. A club's first objective is to survive, and until now the Arctic Council has succeeded in this goal by projecting unity as it steels to fulfil its mandate, while balancing external interests and pressures on both the club and its core club members. In so doing, it has achieved the status of the pre-eminent forum for the Arctic region. Maintaining this status is an essential aspect of the club's efforts at continuation and the club diplomacy that underpins the normative and structural dynamics of its daily practices.

FUTURE RESEARCH

Further research about status in international institutions and forums is needed. While there is a growing body of research on states in pecking orders within institutions and forums, there is less scholarship on how non-governmental organizations and intergovernmental organizations rank within hierarchies traditionally dominated by states, and on the impact of these hierarchies on decision-making processes. Interesting areas in which this research could be expanded include investigating ways to determine how these non-state actors rank in pecking orders compared to other non-state actors, and how they influence the practices of forums and institutions. Institutions that warrant further evaluation of this sort include the International Whaling Commission, which has many non-state actors involved in its work, and the International Maritime Organization, which plays a substantial role in maritime governance. Along the same lines, one could ask how non-state actors influence the work of other clubs and how non-state actors obtain membership (even conditional membership) and rank compared to other club members in clubs.

In the Arctic Council, further evaluation is needed of the pecking orders and practices of the Permanent Participants. They are technically non-governmental organizations, but their special status is embedded in the forum's structures, given that they are made up of and represent Indigenous peoples. They are quite interesting and complex organizations that warrant further evaluation and consideration of how they influence decision-making within their homelands and within the Arctic Council. Do certain branches of the organizations wield greater influence on their work and organization positions? For example, five of the six Permanent Participants (Russian Association of Indigenous Peoples of the North – RAIPON – being the exception) are made up of one overarching group of Indigenous peoples represented in multiple states. Can we evaluate hierarchies among the Permanent Participants in the same way as we do among states? What differences must researchers account for when analyzing the status and role of these organizations? Similarly, what are the relative positions of the Permanent Participants when ranked against each other, and would it be possible to include them on a par with the Arctic states when ranking placements within pecking orders among all the permanent members of the Arctic Council or must they be excluded and accounted for in other ways?

These questions about the participation of the Permanent Participants have unclear answers now and are under-investigated in the academic literature on the Arctic Council. There is little doubt that the Permanent Participants have status and influence, both internally within their organizations and in relation to each other. The details, however, are missing and need to be investigated and unpacked to truly comprehend their capacity to direct diplomacy and decision-making within Arctic governance. Ultimately, more data collection and analytical tools which can account for the structures of the Permanent Participants and the variations in their practices are needed in order to contribute further to an evaluation of the practices, diplomacy, and hierarchies of these club members.

List of Interviews Referenced

1 An academic, 16 September 2016
2 Arctic state politician, 20 September 2016
3 Consultant to the Arctic Council, 14 June 2016
4 Former Arctic Council chair, 2 September 2016
5 Former Arctic Council negotiator, 29 August 2016
6 Former representative to the Arctic Council, 10 May 2016
7 Former representative to the Arctic Council, 11 May 2016
8 Former representative to the Arctic Council, 2 September 2016[1]
9 Former representative to the Arctic Council, 12 October 2016
10 Group interview (three people) with Arctic/Russian research specialists, 14 October 2016
11 Government representative in an Arctic state, 14 September 2016
12 NGO representative, 24 November 2016
13 Permanent Participant representative, 24 May 2016
14 Permanent Participant representative, 25 May 2016
15 Permanent Participant representative, 5 September 2016
16 Representative to the Arctic Council, 21 February 2017
17 Representative to the Arctic Council, 10 May 2016
18 Representative to the Arctic Council, 11 May 2016
19 Representative to the Arctic Council, 12 May 2016
20 Representative to the Arctic Council, 30 May 2016
21 Representative to the Arctic Council, 19 May 2017
22 Representative to the Arctic Council, 21 June 2016
23 Representative to the Arctic Council, 7 September 2016
24 Representative to the Arctic Council, 14 September 2016[2]
25 Representative to the Arctic Council, 15 September 2016
26 Representative to the Arctic Council, 8 September 2017
27 Representative to the Arctic Council, 13 October 2016

28 Representative to the Arctic Council, 14 October 2016
29 Representative to the Arctic Council, 14 November 2016
30 Representative to the Arctic Council, 15 November 2016
31 Representative to the Arctic Council, 24 November 2016
32 Representative to the Arctic Council, 1 November 2017
33 Retired Arctic Council chairperson, 7 June 2016
34 Retired diplomat, 9 May 2016
35 Retired diplomat, 11 May 2016[3]
36 Working group researchers (two interviewees), 26 October 2016

NOTES

1   This is the second of two separate interviews conducted on 2 September 2016.

2   This is the second of two separate interviews conducted on 14 September 2016, the other being with a government representative for an Arctic state.

3   This is the second of two separate interviews conducted on 11 May 2016.

Working Group Chairs

VERIFIED LIST OF WORKING GROUP CHAIRS

	Year	*Country*	*Chairperson*
PAME	1996–2000	Canada	John Karau
	2000–2002	USA	Tom Laughlin
	2002–2004	Iceland	David Egilson
	2004–2006	Kingdom of Denmark	Frank Sonne
	2006–2009	Canada	Chris Cuddy
	2009–2011	Norway	Atle Fretheim
	2011–2012	Iceland	Magnus Johannesson
	2013	USA	Elizabeth McLanahan
	2013–2015	Iceland	Hugi Olafsson
	2015–2019	Canada	Renée Sauvé
SDWG	1996–1998* Not formally a WG until 1998	Canada	Bernard Funston
	1998–2000	USA	Ray Arnaudo
	2000–2002	Finland	Sauli Rouhinen
	2002–2004	Iceland	Hugi Ólafsson
	2004–2006	Russia	Boris Morgunov
	2006–2009	Norway	Stein Paul Rosenberg
	2009–2011	Kingdom of Denmark	Marianne Lykke Thomsen
	2011–2013	Sweden	Mikael Anzén
	2013–2015**	Canada	Sarah Cox (initially but stepped down for medical reasons) Jutta Wark (replacement)
	2015–2017***	USA	Roberta Burns (until Sept 2016, then maternity leave until January 2017 when she returned) Ann Meceda (Sept 2016–Jan 2017)
	2017–2019	Finland	Pekka Shemeikka
AMAP	1991–1993 (Pre-AC)	Finland (?)	Heikki Sisula
	1993–1997	Canada	David P. Stone
	1997–1998	Sweden	Lars-Erik Liljelund
	1998–2001	Kingdom of Denmark	Hanne Petersen

Year	Country	Chairperson
2001–2004	Iceland	Helgi Jensson
2005–2009	USA	John Calder
2009–2013	Canada	Russel Shearer
2013–2015	Kingdom of Denmark	Morten Skovgaard Olsen
2015–2017	Finland	Martin Forsius
2017–Present	Norway	Marianne Kroglund

	Year	Country	Chairperson
CAFF	1992–1993	USA	Dave Allan
	1993–1994	Iceland	Ævar Petersen
	1994–1995	Russia	Amirkhan Amirkhanov
	1996–1997	Kingdom of Denmark	Peter Nielsen
	1998–1999	Canada	Kevin McCormick
	1999–2001	Norway	Berit Lein
	2001–2002	Sweden	Sune Solberg
	2003–2004	USA	Kent Wohl
	2005–2006	Finland	Esko Jaakkola
	2007–2009	Kingdom of Denmark	Inge Thaulow
	2010–2011	Iceland	Ævar Petersen
	2011–2013	Russia	Evgeny Shirikovsky
	2013–2015	Canada	Risa Smith
	2015–2017	Norway	Reidar Hindrum
	2017–2019	USA	Cynthia Jacobson
ACAP	*No Verified Data*	*No Verified Data*	*No Verified Data*
EPPR	*No Verified Data*	*No Verified Data*	*No Verified Data*

UNVERIFIED LIST OF WORKING GROUP CHAIRS

	Year	Country	Chairperson
EPPR	1998–2003	Finland	Olli Pahkala
	2003–2005	Canada	Laura Johnston
	2005–2006	Russia	Igor Verelov
	2006–2007	Norway	Tor Christian Sletner
	2007–2009	Norway	Johan Marius Ly
	2009–2010	USA	Ann Heinrich
	2010–2015	Norway	Ole Kristian Bjerkemo
	2015–2017	USA	Amy A. Merten
	2018–2019	Kingdom of Denmark	Jens Peter Holst–Andersen
ACAP	2004–2008	USA	Bob Dyer
	2008–2012	Russia	Andrey Peshkov
	2012	Finland	Timo Seppälä
	2012–2014	Finland	Jaakko Henttonen
	2014–2015	Sweden	Ann–Sofi Israelson
	2015–2019	Sweden	Ulrik Westman

References

Adler-Nissen, Rebecca, and Vincent Pouliot. 2014. "Power in Practice: Negotiating the International Intervention in Libya." *European Journal of International Relations* 20 (4): 889–911.

Aggestam, Karin, and Ann E. Towns, eds. 2018. *Gendering Diplomacy and International Negotiation*. Cham: Palgrave Macmillan.

AMAP: Arctic Climate Impact Assessment. n.d. "Arctic Climate Impact Assessment (ACIA). "Arctic Climate Impact Assessment (ACIA)." Accessed 24 January 2019. https://www.amap.no/arctic-climate-impact-assessment-acia.

Allport, Rowan. 2017. "Fire and Ice: The Defence of Norway and NATO's Northern Flank." *Human Security Centre*. Accessed 2 April 2017. http://www.hscentre.org/uncategorized/fire-and-ice-the-defence-of-norway-and-natos-northern-flank/.

Arctic Athabaskan Council. 2007. "Improving the Efficiency and Effectiveness of the Arctic Council: A Discussion Paper." 1–10 March. Accessed 1 January 2019. https://oaarchive.arctic-council.org/bitstream/handle/11374/694/ACSAO-NO01_10_1_AAC_AC_Future.pdf?sequence=1–.

Arctic Circle. n.d. "About." Accessed 24 January 2019. http://www.arcticcircle.org/about/about/.

Arctic Council. 1996. "Declaration on the Establishment of the Arctic Council: Joint Communiqué of the Governments of the Arctic Countries on the Establishment of the Arctic Council." 19 September. Ottawa, Canada.

– 2011a. Agreement on Cooperation on Aeronautical and Maritime Search and Rescue in the Arctic. Accessed 24 January 2019. https://oaarchive.arctic-council.org/handle/11374/531.

– 2011b. "Russia Allocates EUR 10M Toward Pollution Prevention Initiatives." 6 October. Accessed 18 October 2017. http://arctic-council.org/index.php/en/component/content/article?id=61:psi-agreement-russia.

– 2013a. "Arctic Council Observer Manual for Subsidiary Bodies." Revised by the Arctic Council at the Eighth Arctic Council Ministerial Meeting, Kiruna, Sweden, 15 May 2013.

– 2013b. "Arctic Council Rules of Procedure." Revised by the Arctic Council at the Eighth Arctic Council Ministerial Meeting, Kiruna, Sweden, 15 May 2013. Accessed 24 January 2019. http://www.sdwg.org/wp-content/uploads/2015/11/2015-09-01_Rules_of_Procedure_website_version.pdf.

– 2013c. "Arctic Council Secretariat Annual Report 2013." 1–34. Accessed 24 January 2019. https://oaarchive.arcticcouncil.org/bitstream/handle/11374/941/ACS_Annual_Report_2013_as_printed.pdf?sequence=1&isAllowed=y.

– 2013d. "Press Release: Welcome to the Arctic Council Ministerial Meeting." Accessed 16 October 2017. http://www.arctic-council.org/index.php/en/our-work2/8-news-and-events/156-press-release-welcome-to-the-arctic-council-ministerial-meeting-2.

– 2015a. "About us." Accessed 24 January 2019. https://www.arctic-council.org/index.php/en/about-us.

– 2015b. "Arctic Contaminants Action Program (ACAP)." Accessed 24 January 2019. http://arctic-council.org/index.php/en/about-us/working-groups/acap.

– 2015c. "Arctic Council Observer Manual for Subsidiary Bodies: Addendum." Approved by the Senior Arctic Officials at the Meeting of the Senior Arctic Officials, Anchorage, United States of America, 20–22 October 2015.

– 2015d. "Arctic Monitoring and Assessment Programme (AMAP)." Accessed 24 January 2019. http://arctic-council.org/index.php/en/about-us/working-groups/amap.

– 2015e. "Conservation of Arctic Flora and Fauna (CAFF)." Accessed 24

January 2019. http://arctic-council.org/index.php/en/about-us/working-groups/caff.

– 2015f. "Emergency Prevention, Preparedness and Response (EPPR)." Accessed 24 January 2019. http://arctic-council.org/index.php/en/about-us/working-groups/eppr.

– 2015g. "Observers." Accessed 24 January 2019. http://www.arctic-council.org/index.php/en/about-us/arctic-council/observers.

– 2015h. "Permanent Participants." Accessed 18 October 2017. http://www.arctic-council.org/index.php/en/about-us/permanent-participants.

– 2015i. "Protection of the Arctic Marine Environment (PAME)." Accessed 24 January 2019. http://arctic-council.org/index.php/en/about-us/working-groups/pame.

– 2015j. "Sustainable Development Working Group (SWGD)." Accessed 24 January 2019. https://arctic-council.org/index.php/en/about-us/working-groups/sdwg.

– 2015k. "Task Force on Arctic Marine Oil Pollution Prevention (TFOPP)." Accessed 1 January 2018. https://www.arctic-council.org/index.php/en/task-forces/67-tfopp.

– 2015l. "Working Groups." Accessed 25 September 2017. http://arctic-council.org/index.php/en/about-us/working-groups.

– 2017a. "Opportunities for Observer Engagement in AC Working Group Activities." SAO Meeting, 5–6 October 2016, Portland, Maine, United States. Accessed 1 January 2018. https://oaarchive.arctic-council.org/handle/11374/1831.

– 2017b. "Senior Arctic Officials' Report to Ministers." SAO Report to Ministers, Fairbanks, Alaska, United States, 11 May 2017.

Arctic Council Indigenous Peoples' Secretariat. n.d. "About IPS." Accessed 1 December 2018. https://www.arcticpeoples.com/about/#bio.

Arctic Council Open Access Repository. 2009. "Update on PSI – Arctic Council's Project Support Instrument." SAO Meeting, 12–13 November 2009, Copenhagen, Denmark. Denmark Chairmanship 1 (April 2009–May 2011). Accessed 24 April 2018. http://hdl.handle.net/11374/962.

– 2014. "Agenda 7.4 Update on the Arctic Council Project Support

Instrument (PSI)." Accessed 17 September 2019. http://hdl.handle.net
/11374/1388.

– 2016. "Arctic Council funding: An overview." SAO Meeting, 16–17
March 2016, USA Chairmanship II (April 2015–17). Accessed 24
April 2018. http://hdl.handle.net/11374/1721.

Arctic Council Open Repository. n.d. Accessed 30 May 2018.
https://oaarchive.arctic-council.org/.

Arctic Council SAO Plenary Meeting. 2016. "Arctic Council Funding:
An Overview." 16–17 March 2016. EDoc code: ACSAOUS202, 1–16.

Arctic Council Secretariat Preliminary 2015 Annual Report. 2016. *Arctic
Council Open Access Repository*, SAO Meeting, 16–17 March 2016, Fairbanks, USA. 1–46. Accessed 24 April 2018. https://oaarchive.arctic-
council.org/handle/11374/1720.

Arctic Council Secretariat. 2015. "Arctic Council Secretariat Annual
Report 2015." Fram Centre: Tromsø.

Arctic Ocean Conference. 2008. "2008 Ilulissat Declaration." Accessed 20
January 2019. https://cil.nus.edu.sg/wp-content/uploads/formidable
/18/2008-Ilulissat-Declaration.pdf.

Argote, Linda. 2013. *Organizational Learning: Creating, Retaining and
Transferring Knowledge*. Boston: Springer.

Åtland, Kristian. 2008a. "Mikhail Gorbachev, the Murmansk Initiative,
and the Desecuritization of Interstate Relations in the Arctic." *Cooperation and Conflict* 43 (3): 289–311.

– 2008b. "Interstate Relations in the Arctic: An Emerging Security
Dilemma?" *Comparative Strategy* 33 (2): 145–66.

Badie, Bertrand. 2012. *Diplomacy of Connivance*. New York: Palgrave
Macmillan.

Baker, Peter. 2014. "If Not a Cold War, a Return to a Chilly Rivalry."
New York Times, 19 March. Section A, 1.

BBC NEWS. 2007. "Russia plants flag under N Pole." *BBC News*, 2 August.
http://news.bbc.co.uk/1/hi/world/europe/6927395.stm.

Bergh, Kristofer. 2012. "The Arctic Politics of Canada and the United
States: Domestic Motives and International Context." *SIPRI Insights on
Peace and Security*, No. 2012/1.

Berthiaume, Lee. 2014. "Ukrainians in Canada Could be Game-Changers
in Federal Election." *Postmedia News*, 5 March. http://www.canada

.com/Ukrainians+Canada+could+game+changers+federal+election
/9578956/story.html.

Blank, Stephen. 2017. "The Bloom Comes off the Arctic Rose." 20 July. *Eurasia Daily Monitor* 14 (96): n.p. https://jamestown.org/program
/the-bloom-comes-off-the-arctic-rose/.

Blaschke, Anne M. 2016. "Running the Cold War: Gender, Race, and Track in Cultural Diplomacy, 1955–75." *Diplomatic History* 40 (5): 826–44.

Bloom, Evan T. 1999. "Establishment of the Arctic Council." Office of the Legal Adviser at the U.S. Department of State. Accessed 18 October 2017. https://2009-2017.state.gov/e/oes/ocns/opa/arc/ac
/establishmentarcticcouncil/index.htm.

– 2009. "Introductory Note to United States Directive on Arctic Policy and the Ilulissat Declaration." *International Legal Materials* 48 (2): 370–3.

Blum, Yehuda Z. 2005. "Proposals for UN Security Council Reform." *The American Journal of International Law* 99 (3): 632–49.

Brady, Anne-Marie. 2017. *China as a Polar Great Power*. Cambridge: Cambridge University Press.

Buchanan, James M. 1965. "An economic theory of clubs." *Economica* 32 (125): 1–14.

Burke, Danita Catherine. 2015. "Marlene Laruelle, Russia's Arctic Strategies and the Future of the Far North." Review of *Russia's Arctic Strategies and the Future of the Far North*, by Marlene Laruelle. *Intelligence and National Security* 31 (3): 456–9.

– 2017a. "Brat opvågning for Danmark: Samarbejdet med Grønland skal forbedres, hvis vi vil være en arktisk nation." In *Politologisk Årbog*, edited by Carsten Jensen, Caroline Howard Grøn, and Caroline Burchardt, 36–41. Hans Reitzels Forlag. http://ibog3.gyldendal.dk
/Politologiskaarsbog2016_2017#/double/1/

– 2017b. "Leading by Example: Canada and its Arctic Stewardship Role." *International Journal of Public Policy* 13 (½): 36–52.

– 2018. *International Disputes and Cultural Ideas in the Canadian Arctic: Arctic Sovereignty in the National Consciousness*. London: Palgrave Macmillan.

– 2019. "Club Diplomacy in the Arctic." *Global Governance* 25 (2): 304–28.

Burke, Danita Catherine, and Teale N. Phelps Bondaroff. 2019. "Becoming an Arctic Council NGO Observer." *Polar Record* 54 (5–6): 349–59.

Burke, Danita Catherine, and Jon Rahbek-Clemmensen. 2017. "Debating the Arctic during the Ukraine Crisis – comparing Arctic state identities and media discourses in Canada and Norway." *Polar Journal* 7 (2): 391–409.

Burke, Danita Catherine, and Andre Saramago. 2018. "Singapore's Use of Education as a Soft Power Tool in Arctic Cooperation." *Asian Survey* 58 (5): 920–41.

Campion-Smith, Bruce, and Alex Boutilier. 2015. "A Conservative Collection of Harper Government Scandals." *TheStar.com*, 14 August. https://www.thestar.com/news/federal-election/2015/08/14/a-conservative-collection-of-harper-government-scandals.html.

Canadian Coast Guard. 2018. "Maritime Search and Rescue (SAR) in Canada." Government of Canada. Accessed 3 January 2018. http://www.ccg-gcc.gc.ca/eng/CCG/SAR_Maritime_Sar.

Canadian Press. 2014. "Canada agrees to work to prevent fishing in High Arctic." *Canadian Press*, 27 February. http://www.cbc.ca/news/canada/north/canada-agrees-to-work-to-prevent-fishing-in-high-arctic-1.2554332.

Carnaghan, Matthew, and Allison Goody. 2006. "Canadian Arctic Sovereignty." Canada's Library of Parliament: Political and Social Affairs Division. Accessed 20 March 2017. http://www2.parl.gc.ca/content/lop/researchpublications/prb0561-e.pdf.

CBC News. 2013. "Leona Aglukkaq becomes first Inuk to helm Arctic Council: Inuit Leaders Applaud Handover of Power." *CBC News*, 15 May. http://www.cbc.ca/news/canada/north/leona-aglukkaq-becomes-first-inuk-to-helm-arctic-council-1.1388905.

– 2014. "Canada Continues Talks with Russia as Part of Arctic Council." *CBC News*, 26 March. https://www.cbc.ca/news/politics/canada-continues-talks-with-russia-as-part-of-arctic-council-1.2587566.

Charturvedi, Sanjay. 2013. "China and India in the 'Receding' Arctic: Rhetoric, Routes and Resources." *Jadavpur Journal of International Relations* 17 (1): 41–68.

Chater, Andrew. 2015. "Explaining the Evolution of the Arctic Council." PhD thesis, School of Graduate and Postdoctoral Studies, University of Western Ontario. Accessed 10 January 2019.

https://ir.lib.uwo.ca/cgi/viewcontent.cgi?article=4566&context
=etd.

– 2016. "Explaining Non-Arctic States in the Arctic Council." *Strategic Analysis* 40 (3): 173–84.

Chunawalla, S.A. 2010. *Mass Communications and Media Studies: Masscommedia.* Mumbai: Himalaya Publishing House.

Coffey, John W., and Robert R. Hoffman. 2003. "Knowledge Modeling for the Preservation of Institutional Memory." *Journal of Knowledge Management* 7 (3): 38–52.

Confucius Institute Headquarters (Hanban). 2014. "About Us." Accessed 15 October 2018. http://english.hanban.org/node_7716.htm.

Conley, Heather, and Caroline Rohloff. 2015. "The New Ice Curtain: Russia's Strategies Reach to the Arctic." Report of the Center for Strategic and International Studies Europe Program. Lanham: Rowman & Littlefield.

Cooper, Andrew F., and Vincent Pouliot. 2015. "How Much Is Global Governance Changing? The G20 as International Practice." *Cooperation and Conflict* 50 (3): 334–50.

Cox, Robert W., and Harold K. Jacobson. 1973. *The Anatomy of Influence: Decision-Making in International Organization.* New Haven, CT: Yale University Press.

De Carvalho, Benjamin, and Jon Harald Sande Lie. 2014. "A great power performance: Norway status and the policy of involvement." In *Small States and Status Seeking: Norway's Quest for International Standing*, edited by Benjamin De Carvalho and Iver B. Neumann, 56–72. London and New York: Routledge.

Depledge, Duncan. 2015. "The EU and the Arctic Council." *European Council on Foreign Relations*, 20 April. Accessed 24 January 2019. http://www.ecfr.eu/article/commentary_the_eu_and_the_arctic _council3005.

Dodds, Klaus and Valur Ingimundarson. 2012. "Territorial Nationalism and Arctic Geopolitics: Iceland as an Arctic Coastal State." *Polar Journal* 2 (1): 21–37.

Dolata, Petra. 2015. "The Arctic: A Diverse and Evolving Region." Berlin: Friedrich Ebert Stiftung, International Policy Analysis, September. Accessed 24 January 2019. https://library.fes.de/pdf-files /id/11640-20151005.pdf.

Dolfsma, Wilfred. 2009. *Institutions, Communication and Values*. Palgrave Macmillan.

Doyle, Alister and Terje Solsvik. 2018. "Greenpeace appeals after losing Norwegian Arctic drilling lawsuit." *Reuters*, 5 February. https://www.reuters.com/article/us-climatechange-norway /greenpeace-appeals-after-losing-norwegian-arctic-drilling-lawsuit-idUSKBN1FP15B.

Embassy of the Republic of Korea in the Kingdom of Sweden. 2013. "Korea gains permanent observer status on Arctic Council." Accessed 24 January 2019. http://overseas.mofa.go.kr/se-en/brd/m _7969/view.do?seq=725701&srchFr=&srchTo=&srch Word=&srchTp=&multi_itm_seq=0&itm_seq_1=0&a mp;itm_seq_2=0&company_cd=&company_nm=.

English, John. 2013. *Ice and Water: Politics, Peoples, and the Arctic Council*. Toronto: Allen Lane.

European Union Science Hub. 2017. "EU and its Arctic partners agree to prevent unregulated fishing in the Arctic Ocean." 7 December. Accessed 6 January 2018. https://ec.europa.eu/jrc/en/news/eu-and-its-arctic-partners-agree-prevent-unregulated-fishing-arctic-ocean.

Exner-Pirot, Heather. 2016a. "Blog: How Much Does the Arctic Council Cost?" *Eye on the Arctic*, 7 September. http://www.rcinet.ca/eye-on-the-arctic/2016/09/07/blog-how-much-does-the-arctic-council-cost/.

–   2016b. "Canada's Arctic Council Chairmanship (2013–2015): A Post-Mortem." *Canadian Foreign Policy Journal* 22 (1): 84–96.

Faulconbridge, Guy. 2007. "Russian sub plants flag under North Pole." *Reuters*, 2 August. https://www.reuters.com/article/idINIndia-28784420070802.

Fenge, Terry, and Bernard Funston. 2015. "The Practice and Promise of the Arctic Council." *Greenpeace*. Accessed 1 January 2018. https://www.greenpeace.org/canada/Global/canada/file/2015/04 /GPC_ARCTIC%20COUNCIL_RAPPORT_WEB.pdf.

Finnish Forest Association. 2017. "Loss of "great northern forest" smallest in Finland, says Greenpeace." 16 March. Accessed 24 January 2019. https://www.smy.fi/en/artikkeli/loss-of-great-northern-forest-smallest-in-finland-says-greenpeace/.

Finnish Government. 2017. "Finnish economy in a phase of rapid growth." Ministry of Finance. Accessed 24 January 2019. http://valtio

neuvosto.fi/en/article/-/asset_publisher/10623/suomen-talous-on-nopeassa-kasvuvaiheessa.

Foighel, Isi. 1979. "Home Rule in Greenland 1979." *Nordisk Tidsskrift for International Ret* 48 (1–2): 4–9.

Fouche, Gwladys. 2017. "Norway environmental lawsuit says Arctic oil plan violates constitution." *Reuters*, 14 November. https://www.reuters.com/article/us-climatechange-norway/norway-environmental-lawsuit-says-arctic-oil-plan-violates-constitution-idUSKBN1DE173.

Gamble, Jim. 2015. "The Arctic Council Permanent Participants: Capacity & Support – Past, Present & Future." *Arctic Yearbook.* http://www.arcticyearbook.com/images/Articles_2015/commentaries/COMM_J_Gamble.pdf.

Gjerde, Kristina M., Harm Dotinga, Sharelle Hart, Erik Jaap Molenaar, Rosemary Rayfuse, and Robin Warner. 2008. "Regulatory and Governance Gaps in the International Regime for the Conservation and Sustainable Use of Marine Biodiversity in Areas beyond National Jurisdiction." *ICUN.* x + 70. Accessed 30 March 2018. https://cmsdata.iucn.org/downloads/iucn_marine_paper_1_2.pdf.

Globe and Mail. 2014. "Canada siding with U.S., Denmark on High Arctic fishing moratorium." *Globe and Mail,* 23 February. http://www.theglobeandmail.com/news/politics/canada-siding-with-us-denmark-on-high-arctic-fishing-moratorium/article17061264/.

– 2014. "Cold War reply in Crimea." *Globe and Mail,* 3 March. A10.

Government of the Kingdom of Denmark. 2011. "Denmark, Greenland and the Faroe Islands: Kingdom of Denmark Strategy for the Arctic 2011–2020." Accessed 24 January 2019. http://library.arcticportal.org/1263/.

Graczyk, Piotr, 2011. "Observers in the Arctic Council – Evolution and Prospects." *The Yearbook of Polar Law Online* 3 (1): 575–633.

– 2012. "The Arctic Council Inclusive of Non-Arctic Perspectives: Seeking a New Balance." Originally presented during "The Arctic Council: Its Place in the Future of Arctic Governance." 17–18 January 2012. Munk-Gordon Arctic Security Program and the University of Lapland, 262–305. Accessed 24 January 2019. https://www.researchgate.net/publication/258286347_The_Arctic_Council_Inclusive_of_Non-Arctic_Perspectives_seeking_a_new_balance.

Graczyk, Piotr, and Timo Koivurova. 2015. "A New Era in the Arctic Council's External Relations? Broader Consequences of the Nuuk Observer Rules for Arctic Governance." *Polar Record* 50 (254): 225–36.

Græger, Nina. 2005. "Norway Between NATO, the EU, and the US: A Case Study of Post-Cold War Security and Defence Discourse." *Cambridge Review of International Affairs* 18 (1): 85–103.

Greaves, Wilfrid. 2015. "Arctic Insecurity and Indigenous Peoples: Comparing Inuit in Canada and Sami in Norway." Presented at the ECPR General Conference, Montreal, Canada, 27 August 2015.

Greenpeace International. 2007. "Finland Forests." 7 March. Accessed 24 January 2019. https://www.greenpeace.org/archive-international/en/campaigns/forests/europe/finland-forests/.

– 2009. "History of Greenpeace campaign to save the whales." 9 January. Accessed 24 January 2019. http://www.greenpeace.org/seasia/ph/What-we-do/oceans/whaling/campaign-history/.

– 2014a. "Iceland and whaling." 20 March. Accessed 24 January 2019. https://www.greenpeace.org/archive-international/en/campaigns/oceans/fit-for-the-future/whaling/icelandic-whaling/.

– 2014b. "Norway and whaling." 20 March. Accessed 24 January 2019. https://www.greenpeace.org/archive-international/en/campaigns/oceans/fit-for-the-future/whaling/norwegian-whaling/.

– 2015. "Greenpeace US activists block Shell's Alaska-bound oil rig." 15 June. Accessed 24 January 2019. https://www.greenpeace.org/archive-international/en/press/releases/2015/Greenpeace-US-activists-block-Shells-Alaska-bound-oil-rig/.

– 2017. "Justice served in Greenpeace Arctic 30 case as Russia ordered to pay the Netherlands €5.4 million in damages." 18 July. Accessed 24 January 2019. https://www.greenpeace.org/international/press-release/7491/justice-served-in-greenpeace-arctic-30-case-as-russia-ordered-to-pay-the-netherlands-e5-4-million-in-damages/.

– 2018. "Decision made in case against Arctic oil in Norway: Right to a healthy environment acknowledged." 4 January. Accessed 24 January 2019. https://www.greenpeace.org/international/press-release/11705/decision-made-in-case-against-arctic-oil-in-norway-right-to-a-healthy-environment-acknowledged/.

Haas, E. 1990. *When knowledge is power*. Berkeley: University of California Press.

Haavisto, Pekka. 2001. "Review of the Arctic Council Structures: Consultant's Study." Arctic Council Open Access Repository, SAO Meeting, 12–13 June 2001 Finland Chairmanship 1 (October 2000–October 2002), Rovaniemi, Finland, 1–55. Accessed 18 October 2017. http://hdl.handle.net/11374/449.

Hardt, Heidi. 2017. "How NATO remembers: explaining institutional memory in NATO crisis management." *European Security* 26 (1): 120–48.

Hart, Robin. 2017. "The soft power of government-funded scholarship schemes – how to measure impact?" *The Association of Commonwealth Universities*. Accessed 24 January 2019. https://www.acu.ac.uk/about-us/blog/soft-power-governmentfunded-scholarship-schemes-how-measure-impact.

Herman, Sondra R. 1995. "Gender, Development, and Diplomacy." *Journal of Women's History* 7 (2): 152–9.

Hilde, Paal Sigurd. 2014. "Armed Forces and Security Challenges in the Arctic." In *Geopolitics and Security in the Arctic: Regional Dynamics in a Global World*, edited by Rolf Tamnes and Kristine Offerdal, 147–65. Oxon: Routledge.

Hillman, A.L., and P.L. Swan. 1979. "Club Participation under Uncertainty." *Economics Letters* 4: 307–12.

– "Club Participation Rules for Pareto-Optimal Clubs." *Journal of Public Economics* 20: 55–76.

Hoel, Alf Håkon. 2014. "The Legal-Political Regime in the Arctic." In *Geopolitics and Security in the Arctic: Regional Dynamics in a Global World*, edited by Rolf Tamnes and Kristine Offerdal, 49–72. Oxon: Routledge.

Hsieh, Hsiu-Fang, and Sarah E. Shannon. 2005. "Three Approaches to Qualitative Content Analysis." *Qualitative Health Research* 15 (9): 1277–88.

Huebert, Rob., Heather Exner-Pirot, Adam Lajeunesse, and Jay Gulledge. 2012. "Climate Change & International Security: The Arctic as a Bellwether." Arlington, Virginia: Center for Climate and Energy Solutions.

Hund, Ian. 2008. "Myths of Membership: The Politics of Legitimation in UN Security Council Reform." *Global Governance* 14 (2): 199–217.

International Whaling Commission. n.d. Accessed 24 January 2019. https://iwc.int/home.

IISD. 2015. "BBNJ Working Group Concludes Mandate, Agrees on Nature of Future Instrument." Accessed 28 June 2016. http://nr.iisd.org/news/bbnj-working-group-concludes-mandate-agrees-on-nature-of-future-instrument/.

– 2017. "Fourth Session of the Preparatory Committee on BBNJ." 10–21 July 2017. Accessed 24 January 2019. http://sdg.iisd.org/events/fourth-session-of-the-preparatory-committee-on-bbnj/.

Ilulissat Declaration. 2008. Arctic Ocean Conference, Ilulissat, Greenland. 27–29 May 2008. Accessed 24 January 2019. http://www.ocean law.org/downloads/arctic/Ilulissat_Declaration.pdf.

Inge, Joseph R. and Eric A. Findley. 2006. "North American Defense and Security after 9/11." *JFQ Forum* 40 (1): 23–8.

Jakobson, Linda. 2010. "China Prepares for an Ice-Free Arctic." *Stockholm International Peace Research Institute (SIPRI) Insight on Peace and Security*, No. 2010/2.

Jakobson, Linda and Peng, Jingchao. 2012. "China's Arctic Aspirations." *Stockholm International Peace Research Institute (SIPRI) Policy Paper*, No. 34 (November).

James, Alan. 2016. "Diplomatic Relations Between States." In *The SAGE Handbook of Diplomacy*, edited by Costas M. Constantinou, Pauline Kerr, and Paul Sharp, 257–67. Los Angeles: SAGE.

Jervis, Robert. 2017. *How Statesmen Think: The Psychology of International Politics*. Princeton and Oxford: Princeton University Press.

Johannsson, Magnus. 2013. "Arctic Council Secretariat Established." *Arctic Yearbook*. https://www.arcticyearbook.com/index.php/commentaries-2013/67-arctic-council-secretariat-established

Josefsen, Eva. 2010. "The Saami and the National Parliaments: Channels for Political Influence." *Inter-Parliamentary Union and United Nations Development Programme*. Accessed 24 January 2019. http://archive.ipu.org/splz-e/chiapas10/saami.pdf.

Kankaapää, Paula, and Oran R. Young. 2012. "The Effectiveness of the Arctic Council." *Polar Research* 31 (1): 1–14.

Käpylä, Juha, Harri Mikkola, and Toivo Martikainen. 2016. "Moscow's

Arctic Dreams Turned Sour? Analysing Russia's Policies in the Arctic." *FIIA Briefing Paper*, 192. Accessed 25 October 2016. https://www.fiia .fi/en/publication/moscows-arctic-dreams-turned-sour-2.

Keating, Joshua. 2014. "The Weird World of International Whaling Rules." *Slate*, 31 March. Accessed 24 January 2019. http://www.slate .com/blogs/the_world_/2014/03/31/icj_whaling_decision_the_weird _world_of_international_whaling_rules.html.

Keskitalo, E.C.H. 2004. *Negotiating the Arctic: The Construction of an International Region*. New York & London: Routledge.

Khrushcheva, Olga, and Marianna Poberezhskaya. 2016. "The Arctic in the political discourse of Russian leaders: the national pride and economic ambitions." *East European Politics* 32 (4): 547–66.

Kim, Ilhyung, and Hae Lim Seo. 2009. "Depreciation and transfer of knowledge: an empirical exploration of a shipbuilding process." *International Journal of Production Research* 47 (7): 1857–76.

Kirchner, Andree. 2000. "The Destructive Legacy of the Cold War: The Dumping of Radioactive Waste in the Arctic." *European Environmental Law Review* 9 (2): 47–55.

Klimenko, Ekaterina. 2016. "Russia's Arctic Security Policy: Still Quiet in the High North?" *SIPRI Policy Paper*, 45 (February).

Koivurova, Timo, and Erik J. Molenaar. 2010. "International Governance and Regulation of the Marine Arctic." *World Wildlife Fund International Arctic Programme*.

Koivurova, Timo, and Md. Waliul Hasanat. 2009. "The Climate Policy of the Arctic Council." In *Climate Governance in the Arctic*, edited by Timo Koivurova, E. Carina H. Keskitalo, and Nigel Bankes, 51–75. Springer.

Kutz, S.F.J., E.P. Hoberg, L. Polley, and E.J. Jenkins. 2005. "Global Warming is Changing the Dynamics of Arctic Host-Parasite Systems." *Proceedings: Biological Sciences* 272 (1581): 2571–6.

Lahn, Bård, and Elana Wilson Rowe. 2015. "How to be a 'front-Runner': Norway and international climate politics." In *Small State Status Seeking: Norway's Quest for International Standing*, edited by Benjamin de Carvalho and Iver B. Neumann, 126–45. Oxon and New York: Routledge.

Larson, Deborah Welsh, T.V. Paul, and William C. Wohlforth. 2014. "Status and World Order." In *Status in World Politics*, edited by T.V. Paul,

Deborah Welch Larson, and William C. Wohlforth, 3–30. Cambridge: Cambridge University Press.

Laruelle, Marlene. 2014. *Russia's Arctic Strategies and the Future of the Far North*. Armonk, NY: M.E. Sharpe.

Laursen, Wendy. 2017. "Norway's Whaling Comes Under Fire." *The Maritime Executive*, 22 March. https://www.maritime-executive.com /article/norways-whaling-comes-under-fire#gs.tI0a79I.

Lebow, Richard Ned. 2006. "The memory of politics in postwar Europe." In *The Memory of Politics in Postwar Europe*, edited by R.N. Lebow, W. Kansteiner, and C. Fogu, 1–39. Durham, NC: Duke University Press.

– 2008. "The Future of Memory." *Annals of the American Academy* 617 (1): 25–41.

Lee, Jack T. 2015. "Soft Power and Cultural Diplomacy: Emerging Education Hubs in Asia." *Comparative Education* 51 (3): 353–74.

Liu, Nengye. 2017. "China-Russia Trouble on the Arctic Silk Road?" *The Diplomat*, 21 July. https://thediplomat.com/2017/07/china-russia-trouble-on-the-arctic-silk-road/.

Loukacheva, Natalia. 2009. "Arctic Indigenous Peoples' Internationalism: In Search of a Legal Justification." *Polar Record* 45 (232): 51–8.

Medby, Ingrid A. 2014. "Arctic State, Arctic Nation? Arctic National Identity Among the Post-Cold War Generation in Norway." *Polar Geography* 37 (4): 252–69.

Min, Pan. 2017. "Fisheries issue in the Central Arctic Ocean and its future governance." *Polar Journal* 7 (2): 410–18.

Ministry of Foreign Affairs Singapore. 2017. "MFA Press Statement: Visit of Minister of State in the Prime Minister's Office and Ministry of Manpower Sam Tan to Norway, 22–25 January 2017." Accessed 23 May 2017. https://www.mfa.gov.sg/content/mfa/media_centre /press_room/pr/2017/201701/press_20170125.html.

Morrow, Weston. 2016. "Fairbanks to Host Arctic Council Ministerial Meeting in 2017." *Daily News-Miner*, 25 January. http://www.newsminer.com/news/local_news/fairbanks-to-host-arctic-council-ministerial-meeting-in/article_60243ed4-c3ae-11e5-9816-c71b2b6f32fa.html.

Murray, Robert W., and Tom Keating. 2014. "Containing Russia should not mean bringing NATO to the Arctic." *Globe and Mail*, 25 April. https://www.theglobeandmail.com/opinion/containing-russia-should-not-mean-bringing-nato-to-the-arctic/article18208720/.

Myers, Steven Lee. 2015. "Arctic Council Meeting Starts Amid Russia Tensions." *New York Times*, 24 April. https://www.nytimes.com/2015/04/25/us/politics/arctic-council-meeting-russia.html?_r=0.

Naalakkersuisut/Government of Greenland. n.d. "Politics in Greenland." Accessed 24 January 2019. http://naalakkersuisut.gl/en/About-government-of-greenland/About-Greenland/Politics-in-Greenland.

NATO. n.d. "Member Countries." Accessed 18 October 2017. http://www.nato.int/nato-welcome/index.html.

NATO Review. 2016. "Sanctions after Crimea: Have they worked?" Accessed 18 October 2017. https://www.nato.int/docu/review/2015/Russia/sanctions-after-crimea-have-they-worked/EN/index.html.

NATO-Russia Council. n.d. "About NRC." Accessed 18 October 2017. https://www.nato.int/nrc-website/en/about/index.html.

Neumann, Iver B. 2008. "The Body of the Diplomat." *European Journal of International Relations* 14 (4): 671–95.

– 2011. "Peace and Reconciliation Efforts as Systems-Maintaining Diplomacy: The Case of Norway." *International Journal* 66 (3): 563–79.

New York Times. 1999. "Norway's Whale Hunters Battle Activists and the Marketplace." *New York Times*, 5 August. https://www.nytimes.com/1999/08/05/world/norway-s-whale-hunters-battle-activists-and-the-marketplace.html.

Nilsson, Annika E. 2012. "Knowing the Arctic: The Arctic Council as a Cognitive Forerunner." In *The Arctic Council: Its Place in the Future of Arctic Governance*, edited by Thomas S. Axworthy, Timo Koivurova, and Waliul Hasanat, 190–224. Munk-Gordon Arctic Security Program and the University of Lapland.

Nord, Douglas. 2010. "The Shape of the Table, The Shape of the Arctic." *International Journal* 65 (4): 825–36.

– 2016. *The Arctic Council: Governance within the Far North*. London and New York: Routledge.

North Atlantic Treaty Organization. 2017. "NATO-Russia Council." Accessed 18 October 2017. http://www.nato.int/cps/en/natohq/topics_50091.htm.

Nye, Joseph S. 2011. "The Future of Power." *Bulletin of the American Academy of Arts and Sciences* 64 (3): 45–52.

Observer Report. 2016. "Observer Report." *Republic of Singapore*.

Accessed 23 May 2017. https://oaarchive.arctic-council.org
/bitstream/handle/11374/1863/EDOCS-4021-v1A-2016-11-30
_Singapore_Observer_activity_report.PDF?sequence=1.

Oceans & Law of the Sea. n.d. "Preparatory Committee established by
General Assembly resolution 69/292: Development of an international legally binding instrument under the United Nations Convention
on the Law of the Sea on the conservation and sustainable use of
marine biological diversity of areas beyond national jurisdiction."
United Nations – Office of Legal Affairs. Accessed 28 June 2016.
http://www.un.org/depts/los/biodiversity/prepcom.htm.

Oglesby, Donna Marie. 2016. "Diplomatic Language." In *The SAGE Handbook of Diplomacy*, edited by Costas M. Constantinou, Pauline Kerr,
and Paul Sharp, 242–54. Los Angeles: SAGE.

Paul, T.V., Deborah Welch Larson, and William C. Wohlforth, eds. 2014.
Status in World Politics. Cambridge: Cambridge University Press.

Pedersen, Torbjørn. 2012. "Debates Over the Role of the Arctic Council."
Ocean Development & International Law 43 (2): 146–56.

Pharand, Donat. 1968. "Soviet Union Warns United States Against Use
of Northeast Passage." *The American Journal of International Law* 62
(4): 927–35.

Phelps Bondaroff, N. Teale, and Danita Catherine Burke. 2014. "Bridging
Troubled Waters: History as Political Opportunity Structure." *Journal
of Civil Society* 10 (2): 165–83.

Phillips, Leigh. 2009. "Arctic Council rejects EU's observer application."
EU Observer, 30 April. https://euobserver.com/environment/28043.

Pieters, Janene. 2015. "Greenpeace calls for Shell Boycott after Alaska
Drilling Go-Ahead." *New York Times*, 18 August 2015. https://nltimes
.nl/2015/08/18/greenpeace-calls-shell-boycott-alaska-drilling-go-
ahead.

Poelzer, Greg, and Gary N. Wilson. 2014. "Governance in the Arctic:
Political Systems and Geopolitics." In *Arctic Human Development
Report: Regional Processes and Global Linkages*, edited by Joan Nymand
Larsen and Gail Fondahl, 185–222. NORDEN.

Pong, Jane, and Emily Feng. 2017. "Confucius Institutes: cultural asset
or campus threat?" *Financial Times*, 26 October. Accessed 24 January
2019. https://ig.ft.com/confucius-institutes/.

Pouliot, Vincent. 2014. "Setting Status in Stone: The Negotiation of

International Institutional Privileges". In *Status in World Politics*, edited by T.V. Paul, Deborah Welch Larson, and William C. Wohlforth, 192–216. New York: Cambridge University Press.

– 2016a. "Hierarchy in Practice: Multilateral Diplomacy and the Governance of International Security." *European Journal of International Security* 1 (1): 5–26.

– 2016b. *International Pecking Orders: The Politics and Practices of Multilateral Diplomacy*. Cambridge: Cambridge University Press.

Pouliot, Vincent, and Jérémie Cornut. (2015). "Practice Theory and the Study of Diplomacy: A Research Agenda." *Cooperation and Conflict* 50 (3): 297–315.

Prime Minister's Office Finland. 2013. "Finland's Strategy for the Arctic Region 2013: Government resolution on 23 August 2013." Accessed 24 January 2019. http://vnk.fi/documents/10616/334509/Arktinen +strategia+2013+en.pdf/6b6fb723-40ec-4c17-b286-5b5910fbecf4.

Quan, H.L.T. 2004. "Race, nation and diplomacy: Japanese immigrants and the reconfiguration of Brazil's 'desirables.'" *Journal for the Study of Race, Nation and Culture* 10 (3): 339–67.

Quinn, Ellis. 2014. "Canada Boycotts Moscow Arctic Council Meeting over Ukraine." *Eye on the Arctic*, 16 April. http://www.rcinet.ca/eye-on-the-arctic/2014/04/16/canada-boycotts-moscow-arctic-council-meeting-over-ukraine/.

Rahman, Talyn. 2011. "Women in Diplomacy: An Assessment of British Female Ambassadors in Overcoming Gender Hierarchy, 1990–2010." *American Diplomacy*, 4 April 2011.

Rayfuse, Rosemary. 2010. "Moving beyond the tragedy of the global commons: The Grotian legacy and the future of sustainable management of the biodiversity of the high seas." In *The Future of International Environmental Law*, edited by David Leary and Balakrishna Pisupati, 201–24. Tokyo: UNNU Press.

Report of the Standing Committee on Foreign Affairs and International Development. 2013. "Canada and the Arctic Council: An Agenda for Regional Leadership." House of Commons Canada, May 2013, 41st Parliament, 1st Session. Accessed 10 January 2019. http://www .ourcommons.ca/Content/Committee/411/FAAE/Reports/RP 6152661/faaerp09/faaerp09-e.pdf.

Rogers, Sarah. 2016. "Arctic fishery meeting makes progress, but no agreement yet." *Nunatsiaq Online*, 13 July. http://www.nunat siaqonline.ca/stories/article/65674arctic_fishery_meeting_makes _progress_but_no_agreement/.

Rosenfeld, Stephen S. 1995. "Ethnic Diplomacy." *Washington Post*, 29 September. A27.

Rossi, Christopher R. 2015. "The club within the club: the challenge of a soft law framework in a global Arctic context." *Polar Journal* 5 (1): 8–34.

Rottem, Svein Vigeland. 2007. "The Ambivalent Ally: Norway in the New NATO." *Contemporary Security Policy* 28 (3): 619–37.

Rowe, Elana Wilson. 2016. "The Arctic in Moscow." In *Sustaining Russia's Arctic Cities: Resource Politics, Migration and Climate*, edited by Robert Orttung, 25–41. New York: Berghahn Books.

Sandler, Todd. 2013. "Buchanan clubs." *Constitutional Political Economy* 24 (4): 265–84.

Sandler, Todd, and John Tschirhart. 1997. "Club Theory: Thirty Years Later." *Public Choice* 93 (3–4): 335–55.

Schaefer, Kai. 2017. "Reforming the United Nations Security Council: Feasibility or Utopia?" *International Negotiation* 22 (2017): 62–91.

Schwartz, Daniel. 2015. "Going Deeper into Canada's 2015 Federal Election Results: New Voters May have been Key Component of Liberals' Victory." *CBC News*, 21 October. http://www.cbc.ca/news /politics/canada-election-2015-numbers-1.3281210.

Sevunts, Levon. 2017. "Arctic nations and fishing powers sign 'historic' agreement on fishery." Radio Canada International, 30 November. http://www.rcinet.ca/en/2017/11/30/arctic-states-and-major-fishing-powers-reach-historic-agreement-on-fishery-in-central-arctic-ocean/.

Shadian, Jessica. 2010. "From States to Polities: Reconceptualizing Sovereignty Through Inuit Governance." *European Journal of International Relations* 16 (3): 485–510.

Statistics Canada. 2016. "Census Profile, 2016 Census." Accessed 24 January 2019. http://www12.statcan.gc.ca/census-recensement/2016 /dp-pd/prof/details/page.cfm?Lang=E&Geo1=POPC&Code1 =0306&Geo2=PR&Code2=61&Data=Count&SearchText=Iqaluit &SearchType=Begins&SearchPR=01&B1=All&wbdisable=true.

Statistics Norway. 2018. "Economic and Financial Data for Norway."

Accessed 24 January 2019. https://www.ssb.no/en/nasjonalregnskap-og-konjunkturer/nokkeltall/economic-and-financial-data-for-norway/.

Steinberg, Philip, and Klaus Dodds. 2015. "The Arctic Council after Kiruna." *Polar Record* 51 (1): 108–10.

Steinberg, Philip E., Jeremy Tasch, and Hannes Gerhardt. 2015. *Contesting the Arctic: Politics and Imaginaries in the Circumpolar North*. London: I.B. Tauris.

Sterbenz, Frederic P., and Todd Sandler. 1992. "Sharing among Clubs: A Club of Clubs Theory." Oxford Economic Papers, New Series 44 (1): 1–19.

Stewart, Ben. 2015. "When Russia declared war on Greenpeace: The story of the Arctic 30 captured on a Gazprom drilling platform and sentenced to years in jail." *The Independent*, 11 April. https://www.independent.co.uk/news/world/europe/when-russia-declared-war-on-greenpeace-the-story-of-the-arctic-30-captured-on-a-gazprom-drilling-10170138.html.

Stokke, Olav Schram. 2013. "The Promise of Involvement: Asia in the Arctic." *Strategic Analysis* 37 (4): 474–9.

Stone, David P. 2015. *The Changing Arctic Environment: The Arctic Messenger*. Cambridge: Cambridge University Press.

Strauss, Nadine, Sanne Kruikemeier, Heleen van der Meulen, Guda van Noort. 2015. "Digital diplomacy in GCC Countries: Strategic Communication of Western Embassies on Twitter." *Government Information Quarterly* 32 (2015): 369–79.

Supreme Court of Canada. 2017. "Clyde River (Hamlet) *v.* Petroleum Geo-Services Inc., 2017 SCC 40." 26 July. Accessed 24 January 2019. https://scc-csc.lexum.com/scc-csc/scc-csc/en/item/16743/index.do.

Tasker, John Paul. 2017. "Supreme Court Quashes Seismic Testing in Nunavut, but Gives Green Light to Enbridge Pipeline." *CBC News*, 26 July. http://www.cbc.ca/news/politics/supreme-court-ruling-indigenous-rights-1.4221698.

Tennberg, Monica. 2010. "Indigenous Peoples as International Political Actors: A Summary." *Polar Record* 46 (238): 264–70.

The Press. 2014. "Old, familiar Cold War chills." *The Press*, 5 March. 16.

The State Council Information Office of the People's Republic of
    China. 2018. "China's Arctic Policy." Accessed 24 January 2019.
    http://www.xinhuanet.com/english/2018-01/26/c_136926498.htm.

The Telegraph. 2013. "China granted permanent observer status at Arctic
    Council." *The Telegraph*, 15 May. Accessed 24 January 2019. https://www
    .telegraph.co.uk/news/worldnews/asia/china/10060624/China-granted-
    permanent-observer-status-at-Arctic-Council.html.

The Trans Arctic Agenda. 2014. "Summary Report: A high-level interna-
    tional seminar at Reykjavik, Iceland, 28–29 October 2014." Accessed
    24 January 2019. http://ams.hi.is/wp-content/uploads/2014/04
    /Trans-Arctic-brochure-A5-2015.pdf.

The World Factbook. n.d. "Finland." Accessed 24 January 2019.
    https://www.cia.gov/library/publications/the-world-factbook/geos
    /fi.html.

– n.d. "Norway." Accessed 24 January 2019. https://www.cia.gov
    /library/publications/the-world-factbook/geos/print_no.html.

Tinline, Phil. 2016. "Too Good to Be Forgotten – Why Institutional
    Memory Matters." *BBC News*, 21 March. http://www.bbc.com
    /news/business-35821782.

United States Coast Guard. n.d. Accessed 24 January 2019. https://www
    .uscg.mil/.

U.S. Chairmanship of the Arctic Council. n.d. Accessed 15 March 2017.
    https://www.state.gov/e/oes/ocns/opa/arc/uschair/index.htm.

U.S. Department of State. 2015. "Arctic Nations Sign Declaration to Pre-
    vent Unregulated Fishing in the Central Arctic Ocean." Media Note,
    Office of the Spokesperson. Accessed 28 June 2016. http://www.state
    .gov/r/pa/prs/ps/2015/07/244969.htm.

– 2017. "Meeting on High Seas Fisheries in the Central Arctic Ocean,
    28–30 November 2017: Chairman's Statement." 30 November.
    Accessed 6 January 2018. https://www.state.gov/e/oes/ocns/opa/rls
    /276136.htm.

– n.d. "Ukraine and Russia Sanctions." Accessed 24 January 2019.
    https://www.state.gov/e/eb/tfs/spi/ukrainerussia/.

– n.d. "U.S. Chairmanship of the Arctic Council." Accessed 24 January
    2019. https://www.state.gov/e/oes/ocns/opa/arc/uschair/.

VanderZwaag, David, Rob Huebert, and Stacey Ferrara. 2001. "The Arc-

tic Environmental Protection Strategy, Arctic Council and Multilateral Environmental Initiatives: Tinkering while the Arctic Marine Environment Totters." In *The Law of the Sea and Polar Maritime Delimita-
tion and Jurisdiction*, edited by Alex G. Oude Elferink and Donald R.
Rothwell, 225–48. The Hague, New York, and London: Martinus
Nljhoff Publishers.

Vasovic, Aleksandar, and Adrian Croft. 2014. "U.S., EU set sanctions as
Putin recognizes Crimea 'sovereignty.'" *Reuters*, 17 March 2014.
https://www.reuters.com/article/us-ukraine-crisis/u-s-eu-set-sanctions-
as-putin-recognizes-crimea-sovereignty-idUSBREA1Q1E820140317.

Weidemann, Lily. 2014. *International Governance of the Arctic Marine
Environment: With Particular Emphasis on High Seas Fisheries*. Hamburg:
Springer.

Weiss, Thomas G., and Karen E. Young. 2005. "Compromise and Credi-
bility: Security Council Reform?" *Security Dialogue* 36 (2): 131–54.

Westdal, Chris. 2016. *A Way Ahead with Russia*. Calgary: Canadian Global Affairs Institute.

Whigham, Nick. 2016. "The new cold war: China's creeping ambitions
in the Arctic set the stage for icy showdown." *News.com.au*, 21 November. http://www.news.com.au/technology/environment/natural-
wonders/the-new-cold-war-chinas-creeping-ambitions-in-the-arctic-
set-the-stage-for-icy-showdown/news-story/753e74bed12c666581
18b25ce7c36e56.

Winters, Jeffrey A., and Benjamin I. Page. 2009. "Oligarchy in the United
States?" *Perspectives on Politics* 7 (4): 731–51.

Wright, Glen, Julien Rochette, Elisabeth Druel, and Kristina Gjerde.
2016. "The Long and Winding Road Continues: Towards a New
Agreement on High Seas Governance." *Institut du développement
durable et des relations internationales* (IDDRI) No. 1, March 2016.

Yang, Jian. 2016. "The Arctic Governance and the Interactions between
Arctic and Non-Arctic Countries." In *Asian Countries and the Arctic
Future*, edited by Leiv Lunde, Yang Jian, and Iselin Stensdal, 35–50.
New Jersey: World Scientific.

Zerehi, Sima Sahar. 2016. "10 nations gather in Iqaluit for Arctic
fisheries negotiations." *CBC News*, 6 July. http://www.cbc.ca/news
/canada/north/arctic-fisheries-international-meeting-iqaluit-1.3666217.

Index